D1322467

**Everyman's Poetry**

*Everyman, I will go with thee,*
*and be thy guide*

# Edgar Allan Poe

Selected and edited by RICHARD GRAY

University of Essex

EVERYMAN
J. M. Dent · London

J. M. Dent
Orion Publishing Group
Orion House
5 Upper St Martin's Lane
London WC2H 9EA

Typeset by Deltatype Ltd, Ellesmere Port, Cheshire
Printed in Great Britain by
The Guernsey Press Co. Ltd, Guernsey, C.I.

British Library Cataloguing-in-Publication
Data is available upon request.

ISBN 0 460 87804 2

# Contents

**Essays**

# Note on the Author and Editor

EDGAR ALLAN POE was born in Boston, Massachusetts in 1809 to travelling actors. He had lost both his parents by the time he was two, and was brought up by foster-parents, Mr and Mrs John Allan, in Richmond, Virginia. In 1815 he went with them to England, where he attended school. On returning home, he was sent to the University of Virginia only to be expelled within the year. Mr Allan then wanted Poe to start a commercial career; but Poe was unwilling. He ran away from home and enlisted in the army under a pseudonym. In 1830 he was enrolled at West Point but, in a short while, he was again expelled. Relations with Mr Allan soon broke down completely, and Poe subsequently tried to make his way as an editor, critic, and creative writer. His responsibilities were increased when in 1836 he married his cousin Virginia Clemm, a girl of thirteen. He enjoyed some success with his collection of short stories, *Tales of the Grotesque and Arabesque*, which appeared in 1840; and his poem 'The Raven' caused a sensation when it was published in 1844. However, he was always on the move from one position to another and his financial circumstances were never good. Virginia died in 1847, after a long and painful illness; and Poe turned increasingly to alcohol for support, and to the companion-ship of older women. He died in Baltimore in 1849 in mysterious circumstances, while travelling from Richmond to New York.

RICHARD GRAY is Professor in the Department of Literature at the University of Essex. His books include *The Literature of Memory: Modern Writers of the American South, Writing the South: Ideas of an American Region, American Poetry of the Twentieth Century* and *The Life of William Faulkner: A Critical Biography*. He is the first specialist in American literature to be elected a Fellow of the British Academy.

# Chronology of Poe's Life

| Year | Age | Life |
|------|-----|------|
| 1809 | | Born 19 January in Boston to Elizabeth Arnold Poe and David Poe, Jr |
| 1811 | | Following disappearance of his father and the death of his mother, Poe taken into house of merchant in Richmond, Virginia, John Allan |
| 1815 | 6 | Travels to England with Allan family and attends school in Stoke Newington |
| 1820 | 11 | Returns to Richmond, Virginia |
| 1826 | 17 | Engaged to Sarah Elmira Royster. Enters University of Virginia but leaves after incurring heavy debts. Estrangement from John Allan because of this |
| 1827 | 18 | Assumes the name Henri Le Rennet and travels to Boston. Enlists under the name of Edgar S. Perry in the United States Army. Publishes *Tamerlane and Other Poems* 'by a Bostonian' |
| 1829 | 20 | Death of Frances Allan, his foster-mother. Receives honourable discharge from army. *Al Aaraaf, Tamerlane, and Minor Poems* published in Baltimore |

# Chronology of his Times

| Year | Literary Context | Historical Events |
|------|------------------|-------------------|
| 1809 | Irving, *A History of New York* | James Madison President |
|      |  | Sequoya begins to develop writing system for the Cherokees |
| 1812 |  | Naval war between USA and Britain until 1814 |
| 1814 | Scott Key, 'The Star-Spangled Banner' | Washington DC burned by British troops |
| 1817 |  | James Monroe President |
| 1820 | Irving, *The Sketch Book* | Purchase of Florida from Spain |
|      |  | Missouri Compromise outlaws slavery north of latitude 36 30° |
| 1826 | Fenimore Cooper, *The Last of the Mohicans* | Robert Owen founds community at New Harmony, Indiana |
| 1827 | Fenimore Cooper, *The Prairie* | Disciples of Christ founded by Alexander Campbell |
|      | Audubon, *The Birds of America* (first section; completed 1838) |  |
| 1828 | Webster, *An American Dictionary of the English Language* |  |
| 1829 |  | Andrew Jackson President |
| 1830 | Smith, *Book of Mormon* | Debate in Congress between |

| Year | Age | Life |
|------|-----|------|
| 1830 | | Brief reconcilation with John Allan, during which Poe returns to Richmond. Writes 'To Helen' (p). Enrols in West Point Military Academy |
| 1831 | | Contrives dismissal from West Point. Other cadets help to publish *Poems* by subscription. Writes 'Israfel' (p). First stories written, intended as parodies of *Blackwood's Magazine* Gothic fiction. *Tales of the Folio Club* published |
| 1833 | 24 | Wins prize from *Baltimore Saturday Visitor* with story, 'Ms. Found in a Bottle' (s). Final estrangement from John Allan |
| 1834 | | Death of John Allan, leaving Poe nothing |
| 1835 | | Editor of *Southern Literary Messenger*, a magazine published in Richmond |
| 1836 | | Marries Virginia Clemm, his cousin aged thirteen. Discharged from *Southern Literary Messenger* |
| 1837 | 28 | Moves to New York. Writes his only completed long fiction, 'The Narrative of Arthur Gordon Pym' |
| 1838 | | Moves to Philadelphia |
| 1839 | | Writes 'The Fall of the House of Usher' (s). Associate Editor of *Burton's Gentleman's Magazine*. Publishes *Tales of the Grotesque and Arabesque* |
| 1840 | 31 | Leaves *Burton's Gentleman's Magazine* |

| Year | Literary Context | Historical Events |
|------|------------------|-------------------|
| | | Daniel Webster and Robert Y. Hayne on the nature of the Union |
| 1831 | Montgomery Bird, *The Gladiator* | Nat Turner's slave insurrection in Virginia |
| | | William Lloyd Garrison founds anti-slavery journal *The Liberator* in Boston |
| 1833 | | American Anti Slavery Society founded |
| | | Oberlin College founded as the first co-educational institution of higher learning |
| 1835 | de Tocqueville, *Democracy in America* (vol. 1; vol. 2 1840) | New York *Herald* founded |
| | | Samuel Colt patents his revolver |
| 1836 | Emerson, *Nature* | Texas declares independence from Mexico and establishes the 'Lone Star Republic' |
| | | Battle of the Alamo |
| 1837 | Emerson, 'The American Scholar' Hawthorne, *Twice-Told Tales* | Martin Van Buren President |
| 1838 | | Regular steam travel across the Atlantic begins with arrival of British *Sirius and Great Western* (journey of sixteen days) |
| | | 'Underground railway' for escaped slaves organized by abolitionists |
| 1839 | Longfellow, *Voices of the Night* | Abolitionists found the Liberty Party |
| 1840 | Fenimore Cooper, *The Pathfinder* | Transcendentalist magazine, *The Dial*, founded under the editorship of Margaret Fuller |

| Year | Age | Life |
|------|-----|------|
| 1841 | | Writes 'The Murders of the Rue Morgue' (s) and 'A Descent into the Maelstrom' (s). Editor of *Graham's Magazine*. Increasing health and financial problems |
| 1842 | 33 | Virginia haemorrhages, the first signs of a painful illness that eventually kills her. Writes 'The Oval Portrait' (s), 'The Mystery of Marie Roget' (s), and 'The Masque of the Red Death' (s). Publishes 'The Tell-Tale Heart' (s). Leaves *Graham's Magazine* |
| 1843 | | Wins prize for 'The Gold Bug' (s). Publishes 'The Conqueror Worm' (p). Attempts to publish *The Prose Romances of Edgar A. Poe* in serial form, but first issue fails to sell |
| 1844 | | Writes 'The Purloined Letter' (s). Moves to New York. Joins N. P. Willis's *Mirror* magazine. Publishes 'The Raven' (p) which is an immediate success and is reprinted across the country |
| 1845 | 36 | Co-editor of *Broadway Journal*. Publishes *Tales* and *The Raven and Other Poems*. Writes 'Eulalie' (p). *Broadway Journal* fails. Begins writing a series of articles on 'Literary America' |
| 1846 | | Writes 'The Cask of Amontillado' (s) and 'Ulalume' (p). Moves to Fordham, New York State. Both Poe and Virginia ill |
| 1847 | | Death of Virginia |
| 1848 | | Publishes *Eureka*, a long prose account of his 'philosophy'. Moves to Richmond. Engaged to Sarah Helen Whitman |

| Year | Literary Context | Historical Events |
|------|------------------|-------------------|
| 1841 | Fenimore Cooper, *The Deerslayer*<br>Emerson, *Essays* | New York *Tribune* founded by Horace Greeley<br>William Henry Harrison President. Dies after one month in office; succeeded by John Tyler |
| 1843 | Hickling Prescott, *History of the Conquest of Mexico* | John Smith authorizes Mormon polygamy |
| 1844 | | Telegraph line from Washington to Baltimore opens |
| 1845 | Anna Cora Mowatt, *Fashion; or, Life in New York* | James K. Polk President<br>USA annexes Texas<br>*Scientific American* begins publication |
| 1846 | Hawthorne, *Mosses from an Old Manse*<br>Melville, *Typee* | War between USA and Mexico<br>Mormons under Brigham Young set out for Utah<br>USA acquires Oregon Territory |
| 1847 | Emerson, *Poems*<br>Longfellow, *Evangeline*<br>Melville, *Omoo*<br>Hickling Prescott, *History of the Conquest of Peru* | USA captures Mexico City<br>Salt Lake City founded by Mormons<br>Gold discovered in California<br>More than 200,000 leave Ireland for USA |
| 1848 | Russell Lowell, *The Biglow Papers* (first series) | War between USA and Mexico ends; USA acquires territory between Rocky Mountains and Pacific<br>Free Soil Party founded |

| Year | Age | Life |
|------|-----|------|
| 1849 | 40 | Writes 'For Annie' (p) and 'Annabel Lee' (p). Engaged to Sarah Elmira (Royster) Shelton, to whom he was engaged in 1826. Dies 7 October in Baltimore, Maryland |

(p) = poem        (s) = story

| Year | Literary Context | Historical Events |
|------|------------------|-------------------|
| 1849 | Parkman, *The California and Oregon Trail* Thoreau, 'Civil Disobedience' and *A Week on the Concord and Merrimack Rivers* | Zachary Taylor President William Hunt invents safety pin 'Bloomers' invented by Amelia Jenks Bloomer |

# Introduction

In one of his poems, 'Dreamland', Edgar Allan Poe claims to have reached a strange new land, 'out of SPACE – out of TIME'. That, in a phrase, sums up the simple but radical premise lurking at the heart of all Poe's poetry: the belief that reality does not lie here, in this life. The real, Poe insisted, is not the physical, the material, but its contrary: the spiritual, the intangible. It is the reverse of all that our senses can receive or our reason encompass; and it lies beyond life, something we can discover only in sleep, in madness and trance, or above all in death. It follows from this, Poe felt, that poetry is, or should be, a voyage in search of that fundamentally elusive reality. The best poems, as he saw it, are ones that seek to conjure up, dramatize and discover a world that exists quite separate from the one available to normal consciousness – poems that disclose landscapes of the imagination, unknown to those living merely in the here and now.

These notions, about reality and the true aim of poetry, are most fully articulated in two essays, 'The Poetic Principle' and 'The Philosophy of Composition', in which Poe makes it abundantly clear that the poet should be concerned, first and last, with the 'circumscribed Eden' of his own dreams. 'It is the desire of the moth for the star', Poe says of the poetic impulse in 'The Poetic Principle': 'Inspired by an ecstatic prescience of the glories beyond the grave, we struggle, by multiform combinations among the things and thoughts of Time, to attain a portion of that Loveliness whose very elements, perhaps, appertain to eternity alone'. The poet's task, in effect, is to weave a tapestry of talismanic signs and sounds designed to draw, or rather subdue, the reader into sharing the world beyond phenomenal experience. Poems make nothing happen in any practical, immediate sense, according to this view. On the contrary, the ideal poem becomes one in which the words efface themselves, disappear as they are read, leaving only a feeling of significant absence, of no-thing.

Clearly, Poe drew elements of this visionary, even cabalistic notion of poetry from some of the English Romantics – particularly

Coleridge, whose work he was not above plagiarizing. What is remarkable, however, is just how far he pushed this notion – so that, in his critical hands, the poet becomes a prophet who has somehow seen the promised land and is now trying to lead others there. Or, it could be added, Poe sees the poet as a priest or shaman, using his arts to entice us into a rejection of the here and now – even a kind of magician who is attempting in effect to enchant us, or simply trick us into forgetting the laws of the ordinary world. Seen from this perspective, it is easy to understand why Poe became such an influential figure for Baudelaire and the French Symbolist poets, who learned in part from their American cousin to regard the poet as a person with arcane, almost divine knowledge and the poem as a magic document resisting the heresy of paraphrase. 'The poet makes himself a seer', Rimbaud declared, 'by a long, prodigious, and rational disordering of all the senses'. Poe would undoubtedly have agreed, not least because he would have recognized the echoes of his own essay in these words.

Just how Poe's ideas of poetry shaped his poetic practice is suggested in his essay 'The Philosophy of Composition', where he claims to describe how he came to write his most famous poem, 'The Raven'. The whole piece, he insists, 'proceeded, step by step, with the precision and rigid consequence of a mathematical problem'. Beginning with a decision about length (the poem, he decided, would have to be short enough to create 'unity of impression'), and following this with a choice of 'province' or effect and decisions about the poem's tone and 'key-note' or refrain, Poe claimed that only at a late stage in the process of composition did he consider what, in a narrative sense, 'The Raven' should be 'about'. And, having decided this, he tells us that he then wrote the third stanza from the end before anything else. Poe loved tricks and hoaxes; it was one of the few ways in which his sense of humour found free play (not least because it could work there in conjunction with his ever-present preoccupation with power). And 'The Philosophy of Composition' should be read as a sort of critical hoax, in which the author conceals the literal truth (how he actually wrote 'The Raven') in order to strike at a deeper, symbolic truth (the true genesis of poetry and the proper way in which, in his view, poetry should be read). What matters about 'The Raven', Poe is telling us, is what matters about all his poetry and *all* poetry for that matter: not what is commonly called its 'content' or 'subject' but the elusive, intangible, magical effects the poem creates partly through the *use* of content or subject. Content, narrative or argument or whatever, is merely a means, a device the poet uses while he attempts, coolly and deliberately, to manoeuvre the reader into a state of suspended animation, a sense of the 'glories beyond the grave'. The subject of 'The Raven' did not really matter to me the author, Poe is saying, and it should not really matter to you the reader, either.

Subjects, however, are not neutral elements, even if they are means rather than ends. It matters, after all, what 'wheels and pinions' or 'tackle for scene shifting' the poet adopts to entrance or enchant the reader. Which is all by way of saying that certain poetic scenes and subjects are favourites with Poe precisely because they reinforce his ultimately visionary aims. Unsurprisingly, life after death is a favourite topic, in poems like 'Annabel Lee' or 'The Sleeper'. So, too, is the theme of a strange, shadowy region beyond the borders of normal consciousness: places such as those described in 'The City in the Sea' or 'Eldorado' which are, in effect, elaborate figures for death. As Poe himself explains in 'The Philosophy of Composition', 'the death . . . of a beautiful woman is unquestionably the most poetical topic in the world', precisely because it enhances the seductive nature of death, transforming annihilation into erotic fulfilment. 'O! nothing earthly' begins 'Al Aaraaf', one of Poe's earliest poems – and that captures Poe's narrative thrust precisely: whatever the apparent subject, the movement is always away from the world of things and towards 'nothing'. The sights and sounds of a realizable world may be there in a poem like 'The Raven', but their presence is only fleeting, ephemeral; Poe's scenes are always shadowy and insubstantial, the colours dim, the lighting dusky. In the final instance, the things of the real world are there only to be discarded – as signposts to another country that is, strictly speaking, imperceptible, unrealizable by the waking consciousness.

'Poe's aesthetic, Poe's theory of art,' the contemporary American poet Richard Wilbur has said, 'seems to me insane. To say that art should repudiate everything human and earthly . . . is hopelessly to narrow [its] scope and function.' That is, certainly, arguable. What is surely unarguable is that this theory has profoundly affected the way in which not only poetry but art generally has been perceived in the modern world A brief anecdote can be cited in evidence. Just before the painter Gauguin left Paris for the South Seas, a farewell dinner was held for him. At the dinner, the poet Mallarmé recited 'The Raven' in Gauguin's honour. So struck was Gauguin by the poem that, just a year later, he produced one of his most famous paintings, 'Nevermore', the title of which is borrowed from Poe's haunting refrain. There are a number of visual similarities between poem and painting; but what is far more important is the fact that Gauguin is clearly striving for the same *effect* as the one he received from Poe's lines, the same mysterious feelings. 'I obtain,' Gauguin said,

> by arrangement of lines and colours, using as a pretext some subject borrowed from human life or nature, symphonies, harmonies which represent nothing real in the vulgar sense of the word and which express no idea directly, but which should provoke you to think as music does, without help of ideas or images, simply by the mysterious relationship which exists between our brains and such arrangements of colours and lines.

To this extent, Poe's emphasis on the single and singular state of death is misleading. It obsessed him, of course. But it is worth saying that this obsession led him in the direction that so impressed Gauguin, or for that matter Baudelaire, Mallarmé, Rimbaud and many others: away from the idea of representational art and towards the idea of art as an absolute, purely aesthetic experience. Poetry, writing generally in this context, becomes just one among many possible mediums for realizing and communicating feeling, states of consciousness. The work of art, as Gauguin loftily claims, is not 'about' anything at all; it simply 'is'. It is nature, not physics; a state of being rather than knowing; an experiential process instead of instruction or argument. 'Nevermore' and 'The Raven' have this in common, finally: that they are anti-representational. This, of course, they share with so much art of the late nineteenth and twentieth centuries. It is Poe's peculiar narrowness of focus, on 'nothing earthly', that strikes the reader at first and tends to alienate people like Wilbur. That very narrowness, however, also endows his poetry with a strange, hypnotic quality, making Poe the poet, for all his occasional absurdities, a charismatic figure for so many readers. Closely related to this, it has given Poe a central place in the story of modern poetry, making him one of the founding fathers of Symbolist, Surrealist and Modernist aesthetics.

Poe's American contemporary, Ralph Waldo Emerson, referred to him contemptuously as 'the jingle-man', by which he clearly had in mind Poe's almost obsessive use of repetition, internal and recurring rhyme, drum-beat rhythms and verbal melody all to produce a hypnotic, incantatory effect. The French writer Victor Hugo, by contrast, claimed that he had discovered '*un frisson nouveau*' in Poe's writing; and perhaps when he said this he had in mind not only the elaborate verbal effects that Emerson so disliked but also Poe's tendency to choose words for their mystery or melody rather than their meaning, his use of synaesthetic effects, and his preference for imagery of dream or nightmare. In a way, they were and are both right: a single poem, like 'The City in the Sea', can swing between the obvious and the elusive, the banal and the hauntingly unforgettable, in the space of a few lines. Some of the effects Poe strives for in this poem are both mechanical and obtrusive: the rhetorical building ('Up . . . Up . . . Up'), for instance, and the repetitive rhythms seem to be demanding a response rather than evoking one. Others are simply bad: a line like 'The viol, the violet, and the vine' reads like a pastiche of early Romantic poetry while the use of words such as 'lurid' and 'marvellous' merely points to the reaction Poe wants to elicit from the reader rather than creating the effect itself. And yet, and yet . . . there are lines that haunt the imagination and stay in the memory, and make it clear why Baudelaire, for instance, 'experienced a strange commotion', as he put it, when he first encountered this kind of writing. The description of death looking 'gigantically down' from 'a proud tower', for example, depends precisely on not referring to death directly as proud or gigantic: the transferred epithet adds distance, mystery and fear. Similarly, the portrait of 'turrets and shadows' that 'seem pendulous in air' recollects or anticipates other dream cities, suspended, like Thomas Mann's Venice, in an insubstantial atmosphere of magic. Most notable of all, perhaps, lines such as 'But light from out the lurid sea/Streams up the turrets silently' work by challenging logic. Strictly speaking, light cannot be anything other than silent, so the reference to its silence is at best superfluous. Nevertheless, its very strangeness renders it imaginatively striking: we are being asked, or rather compelled, to look again at the familiar, to gaze on the customarily accepted with wonder and fear. The sense, quietly communicated, is of an impalpable, irresistible force taking over this dream city: a force the very intangibility of which makes it impossible to comprehend, let alone stop.

'Streams up the turrets silently': mystery is the key quality of a phrase like this. At his best Poe *does* achieve an ordered derangement of our senses: he detaches us from the world of phenomenal experience and persuades us of the possibility of other dimensions. To an extent, the absurdities of rhythm and phrasing are all part of it, since they too can often help to discompose the reader, calling into question or even subverting our customary standards of good taste. Poe challenges and unnerves; he reinvents, jettisoning the literal in favour of the imagined, the carefully moulded and mundane in favour of the magical, bare fact in favour of mysterious fantasy. As we read his poems, we see certain experiences and obsessions emerging, haunting almost his every word: death and beauty, alienation and subterfuge, loss and despair, desire and transcendence. What is perhaps most marked, however, is not this or that particular obsession but a guiding impulse: the poetry reveals to us someone who, by sheer effort of will, transforms everything he encounters, who dissolves the sights and signs of the world just as he touches them. The poems of Poe are characterized, above all, by a strenuous effort to re-create reality so that art becomes not so much a mirror as a series of masks, a shuffling off rather than a reflection of the material world. Other writers, American and European, were to feel his influence or even follow his example; or, more simply and disturbingly, they have been haunted by him. But none has gone quite so far in the devising of a craft that thrives on magic and mystery. Poe turned life into shadow play, and poetry into a series of ghostly gestures; in the process, he marked out boundaries for Romanticism and its succeeding movements that few writers have been able, or even perhaps dared, to cross.

RICHARD GRAY

# Edgar Allan Poe

# Tamerlane

Kind solace in a dying hour!
   Such, father, is not (now) my theme –
I will not madly deem that power
     Of Earth may shrive me of the sin
     Unearthly pride hath revell'd in –
  I have no time to dote or dream:
You call it hope – that fire of fire!
It is but agony of desire:
If I *can* hope – Oh God! I can –
  Its fount is holier – more divine –
I would not call thee fool, old man,
  But such is not a gift of thine.

Know thou the secret of a spirit
  Bow'd from its wild pride into shame.
O yearning heart! I did inherit
  Thy withering portion with the fame,
The searing glory which hath shone
Amid the Jewels of my throne,
Halo of Hell! and with a pain
Not Hell shall make me fear again –
O craving heart, for the lost flowers
And sunshine of my summer hours!
The undying voice of that dead time,
With its interminable chime,
Rings, in the spirit of a spell,
Upon thy emptiness – a knell.

I have not always been as now:
The fever'd diadem on my brow
  I claim'd and won usurpingly –
Hath not the same fierce heirdom given
  Rome to the Cæsar – this to me?
    The heritage of a kingly mind,
And a proud spirit which hath striven

Triumphantly with human kind.
On mountain soil I first drew life:
    The mists of the Taglay have shed
    Nightly their dews upon my head,
And, I believe, the winged strife
And tumult of the headlong air
Have nestled in my very hair.

So late from Heaven – that dew – it fell
    ('Mid dreams of an unholy night)
Upon me with the touch of Hell,
    While the red flashing of the light
From clouds that hung, like banners, o'er,
    Appeared to my half-closing eye
    The pageantry of monarchy,
And the deep trumpet-thunder's roar
    Came hurriedly upon me, telling
        Of human battle, where my voice,
    My own voice, silly child! – was swelling
        (O! how my spirit would rejoice,
And leap within me at the cry)
The battle-cry of Victory!

The rain came down upon my head
    Unshelter'd – and the heavy wind
    Rendered me mad and deaf and blind.
It was but man, I thought, who shed
    Laurels upon me: and the rush –
The torrent of the chilly air
Gurgled within my ear the crush
    Of empires – with the captive's prayer –
The hum of suitors – and the tone
Of flattery 'round a sovereign's throne.

My passions, from that hapless hour,
    Usurp'd a tyranny which men
Have deem'd, since I have reach'd to power,
    My innate nature – be it so:
    But, father, there liv'd one who, then,
Then – in my boyhood – when their fire

Burn'd with a still intenser glow
(For passion must, with youth, expire)
    E'en *then* who knew this iron heart
    In woman's weakness had a part.

I have no words – alas! – to tell
The loveliness of loving well!
Nor would I now attempt to trace
The more than beauty of a face
Whose lineaments, upon my mind,
Are – shadows on th' unstable wind:
Thus I remember having dwelt
    Some page of early lore upon,
With loitering eye, till I have felt
The letters – with their meaning – melt
    To fantasies – with none.

O, she was worthy of all love!
    Love – as in infancy was mine –
'Twas such as angel minds above
    Might envy; her young heart the shrine
On which my every hope and thought
    Were incense – then a goodly gift,
        For they were childish and upright –
Pure – as her young example taught:
    Why did I leave it, and, adrift,
        Trust to the fire within, for light?

We grew in age – and love – together –
    Roaming the forest, and the wild;
My breast her shield in wintry weather –
    And, when the friendly sunshine smil'd,
And she would mark the opening skies,
*I* saw no Heaven – but in her eyes.

Young Love's first lesson is – the heart:
    For 'mid that sunshine, and those smiles,
When, from our little cares apart,
    And laughing at her girlish wiles,
I'd throw me on her throbbing breast,

And pour my spirit out in tears –
There was no need to speak the rest –
   No need to quiet any fears
Of her – who ask'd no reason why,
But turn'd on me her quiet eye!

Yet *more* than worthy of the love
My spirit struggled with, and strove,
When, on the mountain peak, alone,
Ambition lent it a new tone –
I had no being – but in thee:
   The world, and all it did contain
In the earth – the air – the sea –
   Its joy – its little lot of pain
That was new pleasure – the ideal,
   Dim, vanities of dreams by night –
And dimmer nothings which were real –
   (Shadows – and a more shadowy light!)
Parted upon their misty wings,
     And so, confusedly, became
     Thine image and – a name – a name!
Two separate – yet most intimate things.

I was ambitious – have you known
     The passion, father? You have not:
A cottager, I mark'd a throne
Of half the world as all my own,
     And murmur'd at such lowly lot –
But, just like any other dream,
     Upon the vapour of the dew
My own had past, did not the beam
     Of beauty which did while it thro'
The minute – the hour – the day – oppress
My mind with double loveliness.

We walk'd together on the crown
Of a high mountain which look'd down
Afar from its proud natural towers
   Of rock and forest, on the hills –

The dwindled hills! begirt with bowers
And shouting with a thousand rills.

I spoke to her of power and pride,
　　But mystically – in such guise
That she might deem it nought beside
　　The moment's converse; in her eyes
I read, perhaps too carelessly –
　　A mingled feeling with my own –
The flush on her bright cheek, to me
　　Seem'd to become a queenly throne
Too well that I should let it be
　　Light in the wilderness alone.

I wrapp'd myself in grandeur then
　　And donn'd a visionary crown –
　　　　Yet it was not that Fantasy
　　　　Had thrown her mantle over me –
But that, among the rabble – men,
　　　　Lion ambition is chain'd down –
And crouches to a keeper's hand –
Not so in deserts where the grand –
The wild – the terrible conspire
With their own breath to fan his fire.

Look 'round thee now on Samarcand! –
　　Is she not queen of Earth? her pride
Above all cities? in her hand
　　Their destinies? in all beside
Of glory which the world hath known
Stands she not nobly and alone?
Falling – her veriest stepping-stone
Shall form the pedestal of a throne –
And who her sovereign? Timour – he
　　Whom the astonished people saw
Striding o'er empires haughtily
　　A diadem'd outlaw!

O, human love! thou spirit given,
On Earth, of all we hope in Heaven!
Which fall'st into the soul like rain

Upon the Siroc-wither'd plain,
And, failing in thy power to bless,
But leav'st the heart a wilderness!
Idea! which bindest life around
With music of so strange a sound
And beauty of so wild a birth –
Farewell! for I have won the Earth.

When Hope, the eagle that tower'd, could see
    No cliff beyond him in the sky,
His pinions were bent droopingly –
    And homeward turn'd his soften'd eye.
'Twas sunset: when the sun will part
There comes a sullenness of heart
To him who still would look upon
The glory of the summer sun.
That soul will hate the ev'ning mist
So often lovely, and will list
To the sound of the coming darkness (known
To those whose spirits harken) as one
Who, in a dream of night, *would* fly
But *cannot* from a danger nigh.

What tho' the moon – the white moon
Shed all the splendour of her noon,
*Her* smile is chilly – and *her* beam,
In that time of dreariness, will seem
(So like you gather in your breath)
A portrait taken after death.
And boyhood is a summer sun
Whose waning is the dreariest one –
For all we live to know is known
And all we seek to keep hath flown –
Let life, then, as the day-flower, fall
With the noon-day beauty – which is all.

I reach'd my home – my home no more –
    For all had flown who made it so.
I pass'd from out its mossy door,
    And, tho' my tread was soft and low,

A voice came from the threshold stone
Of one whom I had earlier known –
  O, I defy thee, Hell, to show
  On beds of fire that burn below,
  An humbler heart – a deeper wo.

Father, I firmly do believe –
  I *know* – for Death who comes for me
    From regions of the blest afar,
Where there is nothing to deceive,
    Hath left his iron gate ajar,
  And rays of truth you cannot see
  Are flashing thro' Eternity –
I do believe that Eblis hath
A snare in every human path –
Else how, when in the holy grove
I wandered of the idol, Love,
Who daily scents his snowy wings
With incense of burnt offerings
From the most unpolluted things,
Whose pleasant bowers are yet so riven
Above with trellic'd rays from Heaven
No mote may shun – no tiniest fly –
The light'ning of his eagle eye –
How was it that Ambition crept,
  Unseen, amid the revels there,
Till growing bold, he laughed and leapt
  In the tangles of Love's very hair?

## To — —

I saw thee on thy bridal day –
  When a burning blush came o'er thee,
Though happiness around thee lay,
  The world all love before thee:

And in thine eye a kindling light
    (Whatever it might be)
Was all on Earth my aching sight
    Of Loveliness could see.

That blush, perhaps, was maiden shame –
    As such it well may pass –
Though its glow hath raised a fiercer flame
    In the breast of him, alas!

Who saw thee on that bridal day,
    When that deep blush *would* come o'er thee,
Though happiness around thee lay,
    The world all love before thee.

# Dreams

Oh! that my young life were a lasting dream!
My spirit not awakening, till the beam
Of an Eternity should bring the morrow.
Yes! tho' that long dream were of hopeless sorrow,
'Twere better than the cold reality
Of waking life, to him whose heart must be,
And hath been still, upon the lovely earth,
A chaos of deep passion, from his birth.

But should it be – that dream eternally
Continuing – as dreams have been to me
In my young boyhood – should it thus be given,
'Twere folly still to hope for higher Heaven.
For I have revell'd when the sun was bright
I' the summer sky, in dreams of living light,
And loveliness, – have left my very heart
In climes of mine imagining, apart

From mine own home, with beings that have been
Of mine own thought – what more could I have seen?

'Twas once – and only once – and the wild hour
From my remembrance shall not pass – some power
Or spell had bound me – 'twas the chilly wind
Came o'er me in the night, and left behind
Its image on my spirit – or the moon
Shone on my slumbers in her lofty noon
Too coldly – or the stars – howe'er it was
That dream was as that night-wind – let it pass.

I *have been* happy, tho' but in a dream.
I have been happy – and I love the theme:
Dreams! in their vivid colouring of life
As in that fleeting, shadowy, misty strife
Of semblance with reality which brings
To the delirious eye, more lovely things
Of Paradise and Love – and all our own!
Than young Hope in his sunniest hour hath known.

# Spirits of the Dead

### 1

Thy soul shall find itself alone
'Mid dark thoughts of the grey tomb-stone –
Not one, of all the crowd, to pry
Into thine hour of secrecy:

### 2

Be silent in that solitude,
    Which is not loneliness – for then
The spirits of the dead who stood
    In life before thee, are again
In death around thee – and their will
Shall overshadow thee: be still.

### 3

The night – tho' clear – shall frown –
And the stars shall look not down,
From their high thrones in the heaven,
With light like Hope to mortals given –
But their red orbs, without beam,
To thy weariness shall seem
As a burning and a fever
Which would cling to thee for ever.

### 4

Now are thoughts thou shalt not banish –
Now are visions ne'er to vanish –
From thy spirit shall they pass
No more – like dew-drops from the grass.

### 5

The breeze – the breath of God – is still –
And the mist upon the hill
Shadowy – shadowy – yet unbroken,
Is a symbol and a token –
How it hangs upon the trees,
A mystery of mysteries! –

## Evening Star

'Twas noontide of summer,
    And mid-time of night;
And stars, in their orbits,
    Shone pale, thro' the light
Of the brighter, cold moon,
    'Mid planets her slaves,
Herself in the Heavens,
    Her beam on the waves.
        I gazed awhile
        On her cold smile;

Too cold – too cold for me –
    There pass'd, as a shroud,
    A fleecy cloud,
And I turn'd away to thee,
    Proud Evening Star,
    In thy glory afar,
And dearer thy beam shall be;
    For joy to my heart
    Is the proud part
Thou bearest in Heaven at night,
    And more I admire
    Thy distant fire,
Than that colder, lowly light.

# A Dream Within a Dream

Take this kiss upon the brow!
And, in parting from you now,
Thus much let me avow –
You are not wrong, who deem
That my days have been a dream;
Yet if hope has flown away
In a night, or in a day,
In a vision, or in none,
Is it therefore the less *gone*?
*All* that we see or seem
Is but a dream within a dream.

I stand amid the roar
Of a surf-tormented shore,
And I hold within my hand
Grains of the golden sand –
How few! yet how they creep
Through my fingers to the deep,
While I weep – while I weep!
O God! can I not grasp

Them with a tighter clasp?
O God! can I not save
*One* from the pitiless wave?
Is *all* that we see or seem
But a dream within a dream?

# Stanzas

How often we forget all time, when lone
Admiring Nature's universal throne;
Her woods – her wilds – her mountains – the intense
Reply of HERS to OUR intelligence!

1

In youth have I known one with whom the Earth
In secret communing held – as he with it,
In daylight, and in beauty from his birth:
Whose fervid, flickering torch of life was lit
From the sun and stars, whence he had drawn forth
A passionate light – such for his spirit was fit –
And yet that spirit knew not, in the hour
Of its own fervour, what had o'er it power.

2

Perhaps it may be that my mind is wrought
To a fever by the moonbeam that hangs o'er,
But I will half believe that wild light fraught
With more of sovereignty than ancient lore
Hath ever told; – or is it of a thought
The unembodied essence, and no more,
That with a quickening spell doth o'er us pass
As dew of the night-time o'er the summer grass?

3

Doth o'er us pass, when, as th' expanding eye
To the loved object, – so the tear to the lid

Will start, which lately slept in apathy?
And yet it need not be – (that object) hid
From us in life – but common – which doth lie
Each hour before us – but *then* only, bid
With a strange sound, as of a harp-string broken,
To awake us – 'Tis a symbol and a token

4

Of what in other worlds shall be – and given
In beauty by our God, to those alone
Who otherwise would fall from life and Heaven
Drawn by their heart's passion, and that tone,
That high tone of the spirit which hath striven,
Tho' not with Faith – with godliness – whose throne
With desperate energy 't hath beaten down;
Wearing its own deep feeling as a crown.

# A Dream

In visions of the dark night
   I have dreamed of joy departed –
But a waking dream of life and light
   Hath left me broken-hearted.

Ah! what is not a dream by day
   To him whose eyes are cast
On things around him with a ray
   Turned back upon the past?

That holy dream – that holy dream,
   While all the world were chiding,
Hath cheered me as a lovely beam
   A lonely spirit guiding.

What though that light, thro' storm and night,
   So trembled from afar –

What could there be more purely bright
  In Truth's day-star?

# 'The Happiest Day,
# The Happiest Hour'

The happiest day – the happiest hour
  My seared and blighted heart hath known,
The highest hope of pride and power,
  I feel hath flown.

Of power! said I? yes! such I ween;
  But they have vanish'd long, alas!
The visions of my youth have been –
  But let them pass.

And, pride, what have I now with thee?
  Another brow may even inherit
The venom thou hast pour'd on me –
  Be still, my spirit!

The happiest day – the happiest hour
  Mine eyes shall see – have ever seen,
The brightest glance of pride and power,
  I feel – have been:

But were that hope of pride and power
  Now offer'd, with the pain
Even *then* I felt – that brightest hour
  I would not live again:

For on its wing was dark alloy,
  And as it flutter'd – fell
An essence – powerful to destroy
  A soul that knew it well.

# The Lake: To —

In spring of youth it was my lot
To haunt of the wide world a spot
The which I could not love the less –
So lovely was the loneliness
Of a wild lake, with black rock bound,
And the tall pines that towered around.

But when the Night had thrown her pall
Upon that spot, as upon all,
And the mystic wind went by
Murmuring in melody –
Then – ah then I would awake
To the terror of the lone lake.

Yet the terror was not fright,
But a tremulous delight –
A feeling not the jewelled mine
Could teach or bribe me to define –
Nor Love – although the Love were thine.

Death was in that poisonous wave,
And in its gulf a fitting grave
For him who thence could solace bring
To his lone imagining –
Whose solitary soul could make
An Eden of that dim lake.

# Sonnet – To Science

Science! true daughter of Old Time thou art!
  Who alterest all things with thy peering eyes.
Why preyest thou thus upon the poet's heart,
  Vulture, whose wings are dull realities?

How should he love thee? or how deem thee wise,
　Who wouldst not leave him in his wandering
To seek for treasure in the jewelled skies,
　Albeit he soared with an undaunted wing?
Hast thou not dragged Diana from her car?
　And driven the Hamadryad from the wood
To seek a shelter in some happier star?
　Hast thou not torn the Naiad from her flood,
The Elfin from the green grass, and from me
The summer dream beneath the tamarind tree?

# Al Aaraaf

### PART 1

O! nothing earthly save the ray
(Thrown back from flowers) of Beauty's eye,
As in those gardens where the day
Springs from the gems of Circassy –
O! nothing earthly save the thrill
Of melody in woodland rill –
Or (music of the passion-hearted)
Joy's voice so peacefully departed
That like the murmur in the shell,
Its echo dwelleth and will dwell –
Oh, nothing of the dross of ours –
Yet all the beauty – all the flowers
That list our Love, and deck our bowers –
Adorn yon world afar, afar –
The wandering star.

'Twas a sweet time for Nesace – for there
Her world lay lolling on the golden air,
Near four bright suns – a temporary rest –
An oasis in desert of the blest.

Away – away – 'mid seas of rays that roll
Empyrean splendour o'er th' unchained soul –
The soul that scarce (the billows are so dense)
Can struggle to its destin'd eminence –
To distant spheres, from time to time, she rode,
And late to ours, the favour'd one of God –
But, now, the ruler of an anchor'd realm,
She throws aside the sceptre – leaves the helm,
And, amid incense and high spiritual hymns,
Laves in quadruple light her angel limbs.

Now happiest, loveliest in yon lovely Earth,
Whence sprang the 'Idea of Beauty' into birth,
(Falling in wreaths thro' many a startled star,
Like woman's hair 'mid pearls, until, afar,
It lit on hills Achaian, and there dwelt)
She look'd into Infinity – and knelt.
Rich clouds, for canopies, about her curled –
Fit emblems of the model of her world –
Seen but in beauty – not impeding sight
Of other beauty glittering thro' the light –
A wreath that twined each starry form around,
And all the opal'd air in colour bound.

All hurriedly she knelt upon a bed
Of flowers: of lilies such as rear'd the head
On the fair Capo Deucato, and sprang
So eagerly around about to hang
Upon the flying footsteps of – deep pride –
Of her who lov'd a mortal – and so died.
The Sephalica, budding with young bees,
Uprear'd its purple stem around her knees:
And gemmy flower, of Trebizond misnam'd –
Inmate of highest stars, where erst it sham'd
All other loveliness: its honied dew
(The fabled nectar that the heathen knew)
Deliriously sweet, was dropp'd from Heaven,
And fell on gardens of the unforgiven
In Trebizond – and on a sunny flower

So like its own above that, to this hour,
It still remaineth, torturing the bee
With madness, and unwonted reverie:
In Heaven, and all its environs, the leaf
And blossom of the fairy plant, in grief
Disconsolate linger – grief that hangs her head,
Repenting follies that full long have fled,
Heaving her white breast to the balmy air,
Like guilty beauty, chasten'd, and more fair:
Nyctanthes too, as sacred as the light
She fears to perfume, perfuming the night:
And Clytia pondering between many a sun,
While pettish tears adown her petals run:
And that aspiring flower that sprang on Earth –
And died, ere scarce exalted into birth,
Bursting its odorous heart in spirit to wing
Its way to Heaven, from garden of a king:
And Valisnerian lotus thither flown
From struggling with the waters of the Rhone:
And thy most lovely purple perfume, Zante!
Isola d'oro – Fior di Levante!
And the Nelumbo bud that floats for ever
With Indian Cupid down the holy river –
Fair flowers, and fairy! to whose care is given
To bear the Goddess' song, in odours, up to Heaven:

> 'Spirit! that dwellest where,
>     In the deep sky,
> The terrible and fair,
>     In beauty vie!
> Beyond the line of blue –
>     The boundary of the star
> Which turneth at the view
>     Of thy barrier and thy bar –
> Of the barrier overgone
>     By the comets who were cast
> From their pride, and from their throne
>     To be drudges till the last –
> To be carriers of fire

(The red fire of their heart)
With speed that may not tire
    And with pain that shall not part –
Who livest – *that* we know –
    In Eternity – we feel –
But the shadow of whose brow
    What spirit shall reveal?
Tho' the beings whom thy Nesace,
    Thy messenger hath known
Have dream'd for thy Infinity
    A model of their own –
Thy will is done, Oh, God!
    The star hath ridden high
Thro' many a tempest, but she rode
    Beneath thy burning eye;
And here, in thought, to thee –
    In thought that can alone
Ascend thy empire and so be
    A partner of thy throne –
By winged Fantasy,
    My embassy is given,
Till secrecy shall knowledge be
    In the environs of Heaven.'

She ceas'd – and buried then her burning cheek
Abash'd, amid the lilies there, to seek
A shelter from the fervour of His eye;
For the stars trembled at the Deity.
She stirr'd not – breath'd not – for a voice was there
How solemnly pervading the calm air!
A sound of silence on the startled ear
Which dreamy poets name 'the music of the sphere.'
Ours is a world of words: Quiet we call
'Silence' – which is the merest word of all.
All Nature speaks, and ev'n ideal things
Flap shadowy sounds from visionary wings –
But ah! not so when, thus, in realms on high
The eternal voice of God is passing by,
And the red winds are withering in the sky!

'What tho' in worlds which sightless cycles run,
Link'd to a little system, and one sun –
Where all my love is folly and the crowd
Still think my terrors but the thunder cloud,
The storm, the earthquake, and the ocean-wrath –
(Ah! will they cross me in my angrier path?)
What tho' in worlds which own a single sun
The sands of Time grow dimmer as they run,
Yet thine is my resplendency, so given
To bear my secrets thro' the upper Heaven.
Leave tenantless thy crystal home, and fly,
With all thy train, athwart the moony sky –
Apart – like fire-flies in Sicilian night,
And wing to other worlds another light!
Divulge the secrets of thy embassy
To the proud orbs that twinkle – and so be
To ev'ry heart a barrier and a ban
Lest the stars totter in the guilt of man!'

Up rose the maiden in the yellow night,
The single-mooned eve! – on Earth we plight
Our faith to one love – and one moon adore –
The birthplace of young Beauty had no more.
As sprang that yellow star from downy hours
Up rose the maiden from her shrine of flowers,
And bent o'er sheeny mountains and dim plain
Her way – but left not yet her Therasæan reign.


PART 2

High on a mountain of enamell'd head –
Such as the drowsy shepherd on his bed
Of giant pasturage lying at his ease,
Raising his heavy eyelid, starts and sees
With many a mutter'd 'hope to be forgiven'
What time the moon is quadrated in Heaven –
Of rosy head, that towering far away
Into the sunlit ether, caught the ray
Of sunken suns at eve – at noon of night,
While the moon danc'd with the fair stranger light –
Uprear'd upon such height arose a pile

Of gorgeous columns on th' unburthen'd air,
Flashing from Parian marble that twin smile
Far down upon the wave that sparkled there,
And nursled the young mountain in its lair.
Of molten stars their pavement, such as fall
Thro' the ebon air, besilvering the pall
Of their own dissolution, while they die –
Adorning then the dwellings of the sky.
A dome, by linked light from Heaven let down,
Sat gently on these columns as a crown –
A window of one circular diamond, there,
Look'd out above into the purple air,
And rays from God shot down that meteor chain
And hallow'd all the beauty twice again,
Save when, between th' Empyrean and that ring,
Some eager spirit flapp'd his dusky wing.
But on the pillars Seraph eyes have seen
The dimness of this world: that greyish green
That Nature loves the best for Beauty's grave
Lurk'd in each cornice, round each architrave –
And every sculptur'd cherub thereabout
That from his marble dwelling peeréd out,
Seem'd earthly in the shadow of his niche –
Achaian statues in a world so rich?
Friezes from Tadmor and Persepolis –
From Balbec, and the stilly, clear abyss
Of beautiful Gomorrah! O, the wave
Is now upon thee – but too late to save!

Sound loves to revel in a summer night:
Witness the murmur of the grey twilight
That stole upon the ear, in Eyraco,
Of many a wild star-gazer long ago –
That stealeth ever on the ear of him
Who, musing, gazeth on the distance dim,
And sees the darkness coming as a cloud –
Is not its form – its voice – most palpable and loud?

But what is this? – it cometh – and it brings
A music with it – 'tis the rush of wings –

A pause – and then a sweeping, falling strain
And Nesace is in her halls again.
From the wild energy of wanton haste
   Her cheeks were flushing, and her lips apart;
And zone that clung around her gentle waist
   Had burst beneath the heaving of her heart.
Within the centre of that hall to breathe
She paus'd and panted, Zanthe! all beneath,
The fairy light that kiss'd her golden hair
And long'd to rest, yet could but sparkle there!

Young flowers were whispering in melody
To happy flowers that night – and tree to tree;
Fountains were gushing music as they fell
In many a star-lit grove, or moon-lit dell;
Yet silence came upon material things –
Fair flowers, bright waterfalls and angel wings –
And sound alone that from the spirit sprang
Bore burthen to the charm the maiden sang:
     "Neath blue-bell or streamer –
       Or tufted wild spray.
    That keeps, from the dreamer,
      The moonbeam away –
    Bright beings! that ponder,
      With half closing eyes,
    On the stars which your wonder
      Hath drawn from the skies,
    'Till they glance thro' the shade, and
      Come down to your brow
    Like – eyes of the maiden
      Who calls on you now –
    Arise! from your dreaming
      In violet bowers,
    To duty beseeming
      These star-litten hours –
    And shake from your tresses
      Encumber'd with dew
    The breath of those kisses
      That cumber them too –
    (O! how, without you, Love!

Could angels be blest?)
Those kisses of true love
  That lull'd ye to rest!
Up! – shake from your wing
  Each hindering thing:
The dew of the night –
  It would weigh down your flight;
And true love caresses –
  O! leave them apart!
They are light on the tresses,
  But lead on the heart.

Ligeia! Ligeia!
  My beautiful one!
Whose harshest idea
  Will to melody run,
O! is it thy will
  On the breezes to toss?
Or, capriciously still,
  Like the lone Albatross,
Incumbent on night
  (As she on the air)
To keep watch with delight
  On the harmony there?
Ligeia! wherever
  Thy image may be,
No magic shall sever
  Thy music from thee.
Thou hast bound many eyes
  In a dreamy sleep –
But the strains still arise
  Which *thy* vigilance keep –
The sound of the rain
  Which leaps down to the flower,
And dances again
  In the rhythm of the shower –
The murmur that springs
  From the growing of grass
Are the music of things –
  But are modell'd, alas! –

Away, then my dearest,
  O! hie thee away
To springs that lie clearest,
  Beneath the moon-ray –
To lone lake that smiles,
  In its dream of deep rest,
At the many star-isles
  That enjewel its breast –
Where wild flowers, creeping,
  Have mingled their shade,
On its margin is sleeping
  Full many a maid –
Some have left the cool glade, and
  Have slept with the bee –
Arouse them my maiden,
  On moorland and lea –
Go! breathe on their slumber,
  All softly in ear,
The musical number
  They slumber'd to hear –
For what can awaken
  An angel so soon
Whose sleep hath been taken
  Beneath the cold moon,
As the spell which no slumber
  Of witchery may test,
The rhythmical number
  Which lull'd him to rest?'


Spirits in wing, and angels to the view,
A thousand seraphs burst th' Empyrean thro',
Young dreams still hovering on their drowsy flight –
Seraphs in all but 'Knowledge', the keen light
That fell, refracted thro' thy bounds, afar
O Death! from eye of God upon that star:
Sweet was that error – sweeter still that death –
Sweet was that error – ev'n with *us* the breath
Of Science dims the mirror of our joy –
To them 'twere the Simoom, and would destroy –
For what (to them) availeth it to know

That Truth is Falsehood – or that Bliss is Woe?
Sweet was their death – with them to die was rife
With the last ecstasy of satiate life –
Beyond that death no immortality –
But sleep that pondereth and is not 'to be' –
And there – oh! may my weary spirit dwell –
Apart from Heaven's Eternity – and yet how far from Hell!
What guilty spirit, in what shrubbery dim,
Heard not the stirring summons of that hymn?
But two: they fell: for Heaven no grace imparts
To those who hear not for their beating hearts.
A maiden-angel and her seraph-lover –
O! where (and ye may seek the wide skies over)
Was Love, the blind, near sober Duty known?
Unguided Love hath fallen – 'mid 'tears of perfect moan.'

He was a goodly spirit – he who fell:
A wanderer by moss-y-mantled well –
A gazer on the lights that shine above –
A dreamer in the moonbeam by his love:
What wonder? for each star is eye-like there,
And looks so sweetly down on Beauty's hair –
And they, and ev'ry mossy spring were holy
To his love-haunted heart and melancholy.
The night had found (to him a night of wo)
Upon a mountain crag, young Angelo –
Beetling it bends athwart the solemn sky,
And scowls on starry worlds that down beneath it lie.
Here sate he with his love – his dark eye bent
With eagle gaze along the firmament:
Now turn'd it upon her – but ever then
It trembled to the orb of EARTH again.

'Ianthe, dearest, see! how dim that ray!
How lovely 'tis to look so far away!
She seem'd not thus upon that autumn eve
I left her gorgeous halls – nor mourn'd to leave.
That eve – that eve – I should remember well –
The sun-ray dropp'd, in Lemnos, with a spell
On th' Arabesque carving of a gilded hall

Wherein I sate, and on the draperied wall –
And on my eye-lids – O the heavy light!
How drowsily it weigh'd them into night!
On flowers, before, and mist, and love they ran
With Persian Saadi in his Gulistan:
But O that light! – I slumber'd – Death, the while,
Stole o'er my senses in that lovely isle
So softly that no single silken hair
Awoke that slept – or knew that he was there.

The last spot of Earth's orb I trod upon
Was a proud temple call'd the Parthenon –
More beauty clung around her column'd wall
Then ev'n thy glowing bosom beats withal,
And when old Time my wing did disenthral
Thence sprang I – as the eagle from his tower,
And years I left behind me in an hour.
What time upon her airy bounds I hung
One half the garden of her globe was flung
Unrolling as a chart unto my view –
Tenantless cities of the desert too!
Ianthe, beauty crowded on me then,
And half I wish'd to be again of men.'

'My Angelo! and why of them to be?
A brighter dwelling-place is there for thee –
And greener fields than in yon world above,
And woman's loveliness – and passionate love.'
'But, list, Ianthe! when the air so soft
Fail'd, as my pennon'd spirit leapt aloft,
Perhaps my brain grew dizzy – but the world
I left so late was into chaos hurl'd –
Sprang from her station, on the winds apart,
And roll'd, a flame, the fiery Heaven athwart.
Methought, my sweet one, then I ceased to soar
And fell – not swiftly as I rose before,
But with a downward, tremulous motion thro'
Light, brazen days, this golden star unto!
Nor long the measure of my falling hours,
For nearest of all stars was thine to ours –

Dread star! that came, amid a night of mirth,
A red Dædalion on the timid Earth.

'We came – and to thy Earth – but not to us
Be given our lady's bidding to discuss:
We came, my love; around, above, below,
Gay fire-fly of the night we come and go,
Nor ask a reason save the angel-nod
*She* grants to us, as granted by her God –
But, Angelo, than thine grey Time unfurl'd
Never his fairy wing o'er fairier world!
Dim was its little disk, and angel eyes
Alone could see the phantom in the skies,
When first Al Aaraaf knew her course to be
Headlong thitherward o'er the starry sea –
But when its glory swell'd upon the sky,
As glowing Beauty's bust beneath man's eye,
We paus'd before the heritage of men,
And thy star trembled – as doth Beauty then!'

Thus, in discourse, the lovers whiled away
The night that waned and waned and brought no day.
They fell: for Heaven to them no hope imparts
Who hear not for the beating of their hearts.

## Romance

Romance, who loves to nod and sing,
With drowsy head and folded wing,
Among the green leaves as they shake
Far down within some shadowy lake,
To me a painted paroquet
Hath been – a most familiar bird –
Taught me my alphabet to say –
To lisp my very earliest word
While in the wild wood I did lie,
A child – with a most knowing eye.

Of late, eternal Condor years
So shake the very Heaven on high
With tumult as they thunder by,
I have no time for idle cares
Through gazing on the unquiet sky.
And when an hour with calmer wings
Its down upon my spirit flings –
That little time with lyre and rhyme
To while away – forbidden things!
My heart would feel to be a crime
Unless it trembled with the strings.


# To —


The bowers whereat, in dreams, I see
    The wantonest singing birds,
Are lips – and all thy melody
    Of lip-begotten words –

Thine eyes, in Heaven of heart enshrined
    Then desolately fall,
O God! on my funereal mind
    Like starlight on a pall –

Thy heart – *thy* heart! – I wake and sigh,
    And sleep to dream till day
Of the truth that gold can never buy –
    Of the baubles that it may.


## To the River —


Fair river! in thy bright, clear flow
    Of crystal, wandering water,
Thou art an emblem of the glow
        Of beauty – the unhidden heart –

The playful maziness of art
  In old Alberto's daughter;

But when within thy wave she looks —
  Which glistens then, and trembles —
Why, then, the prettiest of brooks
  Her worshipper resembles;
For in his heart, as in thy stream,
  Her image deeply lies —
His heart which trembles at the beam
  Of her soul-searching eyes.


## To —


I heed not that my earthly lot
  Hath little of Earth in it,
That years of love have been forgot
  In the hatred of a minute:
I mourn not that the desolate
  Are happier, sweet, than I,
But that you sorrow for my fate
  Who am a passer-by.


## Fairy-Land


Dim vales — and shadowy floods —
And cloudy-looking woods,
Whose forms we can't discover
For the tears that drip all over.
Huge moons there wax and wane —

Again – again – again –
Every moment of the night –
Forever changing places –
And they put out the star-light
With the breath from their pale faces.
About twelve by the moon-dial
One more filmy than the rest
(A kind which, upon trial,
They have found to be the best)
Comes down – still down – and down
With its centre on the crown
Of a mountain's eminence,
While its wide circumference
In easy drapery falls
Over hamlets, over halls,
Wherever they may be –
O'er the strange woods – o'er the sea –
Over spirits on the wing –
Over every drowsy thing –
And buries them up quite
In a labyrinth of light –
And then, how deep! – O, deep!
Is the passion of their sleep.
In the morning they arise,
And their moony covering
Is soaring in the skies,
With the tempests as they toss,
Like – almost any thing –
Or a yellow Albatross.
They use that moon no more
For the same end as before –
Videlicet a tent –
Which I think extravagant:
Its atomies, however,
Into a shower dissever,
Of which those butterflies,
Of Earth, who seek the skies,
And so come down again
(Never-contented things!)

Have brought a specimen
Upon their quivering wings.


## To Helen


Helen, thy beauty is to me
  Like those Nicéan barks of yore,
That gently, o'er a perfumed sea,
  The weary, way-worn wanderer bore
  To his own native shore.


On desperate seas long wont to roam,
  Thy hyacinth hair, thy classic face,
Thy Naiad airs have brought me home
  To the glory that was Greece.
  And the grandeur that was Rome.


Lo! in yon brilliant window-niche
  How statue-like I see thee stand,
The agate lamp within thy hand!
  Ah, Psyche, from the regions which
  Are Holy-Land!


## Israfel


In Heaven a spirit doth dwell
  'Whose heart-strings are a lute;'
None sing so wildly well
As the angel Israfel,

And the giddy stars (so legends tell)
Ceasing their hymns, attend the spell
  Of his voice, all mute.

Tottering above
  In her highest noon,
  The enamoured moon
Blushes with love,
  While, to listen, the red levin
  (with the rapid Pleiads, even,
  Which were seven)
  Pauses in Heaven.

And they say (the starry choir
  And the other listening things)
That Israfeli's fire
Is owing to that lyre
  By which he sits and sings –
The trembling living wire
Of those unusual strings.

But the skies that angel trod,
  Where deep thoughts are a duty –
Where Love's a grown-up God –
  Where the Houri glances are
Imbued with all the beauty
  Which we worship in a star.

Therefore, thou art not wrong,
  Israfeli, who despisest
An unimpassioned song;
To thee the laurels belong,
  Best bard, because the wisest!
Merrily live, and long!

The ecstasies above
  With thy burning measures suit –
Thy grief, thy joy, thy hate, thy love,

With the fervour of thy lute –
Well may the stars be mute!

Yes, Heaven is thine; but this
    Is a world of sweets and sours;
    Our flowers are merely – flowers,
And the shadow of thy perfect bliss
    Is the sunshine of ours.

If I could dwell
Where Israfel
    Hath dwelt, and he where I,
He might not sing so wildly well
    A mortal melody,
While a bolder note than this might swell
    From my lyre within the sky.

# The City in the Sea

Lo! Death has reared himself a throne
In a strange city lying alone
Far down within the dim West,
Where the good and the bad and the worst and the best
Have gone to their eternal rest.
There shrines and palaces and towers
(Time-eaten towers that tremble not!)
Resemble nothing that is ours.
Around, by lifting winds forgot,
Resignedly beneath the sky
The melancholy waters lie.

No rays from the holy heaven come down
On the long night-time of that town;
But light from out the lurid sea
Streams up the turrets silently –
Gleams up the pinnacles far and free –
Up domes – up spires – up kingly halls –

Up fanes – up Babylon-like walls –
Up shadowy long-forgotten bowers
Of sculptured ivy and stone flowers –
Up many and many a marvellous shrine
Whose wreathéd friezes intertwine
The viol, the violet, and the vine.

Resignedly beneath the sky
The melancholy waters lie,
So blend the turrets and shadows there
That all seem pendulous in air,
While from a proud tower in the town
Death looks gigantically down.

There open fanes and gaping graves
Yawn level with the luminous waves
But not the riches there that lie
In each idol's diamond eye –
Not the gaily-jewelled dead
Tempt the waters from their bed;
For no ripples curl, alas!
Along that wilderness of glass –
No swellings tell that winds may be
Upon some far-off happier sea –
No heavings hint that winds have been
On seas less hideously serene.

But lo, a stir is in the air!
The wave – there is a movement there!
As if the towers had thrust aside,
In slightly sinking, the dull tide –
As if their tops had feebly given
A void within the filmy Heaven.
The waves have now a redder glow –
The hours are breathing faint and low –
And when, amid no earthly moans,
Down, down that town shall settle hence,
Hell, rising from a thousand thrones,
Shall do it reverence.

# The Sleeper

At midnight, in the month of June,
I stand beneath the mystic moon.
An opiate vapour, dewy, dim,
Exhales from out her golden rim,
And, softly dripping, drop by drop,
Upon the quiet mountain top,
Steals drowsily and musically
Into the universal valley.
The rosemary nods upon the grave;
The lily lolls upon the wave;
Wrapping the fog about its breast,
The ruin moulders into rest;
Looking like Lethë, see! the lake
A conscious slumber seems to take,
And would not, for the world, awake.
All Beauty sleeps! – and lo! where lies
Irenë, with her Destinies!

Oh, lady bright! can it be right –
This window open to the night?
The wanton airs, from the tree-top,
Laughingly through the lattice drop –
The bodiless airs, a wizard rout,
Flit through thy chamber in and out,
And wave the curtain canopy
So fitfully – so fearfully –
Above the closed and fringéd lid
'Neath which thy slumb'ring soul lies hid,
That o'er the floor and down the wall,
Like ghosts the shadows rise and fall!
Oh, lady dear, hast thou no fear?
Why and what art thou dreaming here?
Sure thou art come o'er far-off seas,
A wonder to these garden trees!
Strange is thy pallor! strange thy dress!
Strange, above all, thy length of tress,
And this all solemn silentness!

The lady sleeps! Oh, may her sleep,
Which is enduring, so be deep!
Heaven have her in its sacred keep!
This chamber changed for one more holy,
This bed for one more melancholy,
I pray to God that she may lie
Forever with unopened eye,
While the pale sheeted ghosts go by!

My love, she sleeps! Oh, may her sleep,
As it is lasting, so be deep!
Soft may the worms about her creep!
Far in the forest, dim and old,
For her may some tall vault unfold –
Some vault that oft hath flung its black
And wingéd panels fluttering back,
Triumphant, o'er the crested palls,
Of her grand family funerals –
Some sepulchre, remote, alone,
Against whose portal she hath thrown,
In childhood, many an idle stone –
Some tomb from out whose sounding door
She ne'er shall force an echo more,
Thrilling to think, poor child of sin!
It was the dead who groaned within.

# Lenore

Ah, broken is the golden bowl! the spirit flown forever
Let the bell toll! – a saintly soul floats on the Stygian river;
And, Guy De Vere, hast *thou* no tear? – weep now or never more!
See! on yon drear and rigid bier low lies thy love, Lenore!
Come! let the burial rite be read – the funeral song be sung! –
An anthem for the queenliest dead that ever died so young –
A dirge for her the doubly dead in that she died so young.

'Wretches! ye loved her for her wealth and hated her for her
    pride,
And when she fell in feeble health, ye blessed her – that she died!
How *shall* the ritual, then, be read? – the requiem how be sung
By you – by yours, the evil eye, – by yours, the slanderous tongue
That did to death the innocence that died, and died so young?'

*Peccavimus*; but rave not thus! and let a Sabbath song
Go up to God so solemnly the dead may feel no wrong!
The sweet Lenore hath 'gone before,' with Hope, that flew
    beside,
Leaving thee wild for the dear child that should have been thy
    bride –
For her, the fair and *debonair*, that now so lowly lies,
The life upon her yellow hair but not within her eyes –
The life still there, upon her hair – the death upon her eyes.

'Avaunt! – avaunt! from fiends below, the indignant ghost is
    riven –
From Hell unto a high estate far up within the Heaven –
From grief and groan, to a golden throne, beside the King of
    Heaven.'
Let no bell toll then! – lest her soul, amid its hallowed mirth,
Should catch the note as it doth float up from the damnéd
    Earth! –
And I! – to-night my heart is light! No dirge will I upraise,
But waft the angel on her flight with a Pæan of old days!


# The Valley of Unrest


*Once* it smiled a silent dell
Where the people did not dwell;
They had gone unto the wars,
Trusting to the mild-eyed stars,
Nightly, from their azure towers,
To keep watch above the flowers,

In the midst of which all day
The red sun-light lazily lay.
*Now* each visitor shall confess
The sad valley's restlessness.
Nothing there is motionless –
Nothing save the airs that brood
Over the magic solitude.
Ah, by no wind are stirred those trees
That palpitate like the chill seas
Around the misty Hebrides!
Ah, by no wind those clouds are driven
That rustle through the unquiet Heaven
Uneasily, from morn till even,
Over the violets there that lie
In myriad types of the human eye –
Over the lilies three that wave
And weep above a nameless grave!
They wave: – from out their fragrant tops
Eternal dews come down in drops.
They weep: – from off their delicate stems
Perennial tears descend in gems.

# The Coliseum

Type of the antique Rome! Rich reliquary
Of lofty contemplation left to Time
By buried centuries of pomp and power!
At length – at length – after so many days
Of weary pilgrimage and burning thirst,
(Thirst for the springs of lore that in thee lie,)
I kneel, an altered and an humble man,
Amid thy shadows, and so drink within
My very soul thy grandeur, gloom, and glory!

Vastness! and Age! and Memories of Eld!
Silence! and Desolation! and dim Night!
I feel ye now – I feel ye in your strength –
O spells more sure than e'er Judæan king
Taught in the gardens of Gethsemane!
O charms more potent than the rapt Chaldee
Ever drew down from out the quiet stars!

Here, where a hero fell, a column falls!
Here, where the mimic eagle glared in gold,
A midnight vigil holds the swarthy bat!
Here, where the dames of Rome their gilded hair
Waved to the wind, now wave the reed and thistle!
Here, where on golden throne the monarch lolled,
Glides, spectre-like, unto his marble home,
Lit by the wan light of the hornéd moon,
The swift and silent lizard of the stones!

But stay! these walls – these ivy-clad arcades –
These mouldering plinths – these sad and blackened shafts –
These vague entablatures – this crumbling frieze –
These shattered cornices – this wreck – this ruin –
These stones – alas! these grey stones – are they all –
All of the famed, and the colossal left
By the corrosive Hours to Fate and me?

'Not all' – the Echoes answer me – 'not all!
Prophetic sounds and loud, arise forever
From us, and from all Ruin, unto the wise,
As melody from Memnon to the Sun.
We rule the hearts of mightiest men – we rule
With a despotic sway all giant minds.
We are not impotent – we pallid stones.
Not all our power is gone – not all our fame –
Not all the magic of our high renown –
Not all the wonder that encircles us –
Not all the mysteries that in us lie –
Not all the memories that hang upon
And cling around about us as a garment,
Clothing us in a robe of more than glory.'

## To One in Paradise

Thou wast all that to me, love,
   For which my soul did pine –
A green isle in the sea, love,
   A fountain and a shrine,
All wreathed with fairy fruits and flowers,
   And all the flowers were mine.

Ah, dream too bright to last!
   Ah, starry Hope! that didst arise
But to be overcast!
   A voice from out the Future cries,
'On! on!' – but o'er the Past
   (Dim gulf!) my spirit hovering lies
Mute, motionless, aghast!

For, alas! alas! with me
   The light of Life is o'er!
   'No more – no more – no more –'
(Such language holds the solemn sea
   To the sands upon the shore)
Shall bloom the thunder-blasted tree,
   Or the stricken eagle soar!

And all my days are trances,
   And all my nightly dreams
Are where thy grey eye glances,
   And where thy footstep gleams –
In what ethereal dances,
   By what eternal streams.

## Hymn

At morn – at noon – at twilight dim –
Maria! thou hast heard my hymn!
In joy and wo – in good and ill –
Mother of God, be with me still!

When the Hours flew brightly by,
And not a cloud obscured the sky,
My soul, lest it should truant be,
Thy grace did guide to thine and thee;
Now, when storms of Fate o'ercast
Darkly my Present and my Past,
Let my Future radiant shine
With sweet hopes of thee and thine!

## To F —

Beloved! amid the earnest woes
   That crowd around my earthly path –
(Drear path, alas! where grows
Not even one lonely rose) –
   My soul at least a solace hath
In dreams of thee, and therein knows
An Eden of bland repose.

And thus thy memory is to me
   Like some enchanted far-off isle
In some tumultuous sea –
Some ocean throbbing far and free
   With storms – but where meanwhile
Serenest skies continually
   Just o'er that one bright island smile.

## To F — s S. O — d

Thou wouldst be loved? – then let thy heart
   From its present pathway part not!
Being everything which now thou art,
   Be nothing which thou art not.

So with the world thy gentle ways,
   Thy grace, thy more than beauty,
Shall be an endless theme of praise,
   And love – a simple duty.


# Scenes from *Politian*


An unpublished drama


1

*Rome. – A Hall in a Palace.* ALESSANDRA *and* CASTIGLIONE.
ALESSANDRA.  Thou art sad, Castiglione.
CASTIGLIONE.                                    Sad! not I.
  Oh, I'm the happiest, happiest man in Rome!
  A few days more, thou knowest, my Alessandra,
  Will make thee mine. Oh, I am very happy!
ALESS.  Methinks thou hast a singular way of showing
  Thy happiness! – what ails thee, cousin of mine?
  Why didst thou sigh so deeply?
CAS.                                    Did I sigh?
  I was not conscious of it. It is a fashion,
  A silly – a most silly fashion I have
  When I am *very* happy. Did I sigh? (*sighing*)
ALESS.  Thou didst. Thou art not well. Thou hast indulged
  Too much of late, and I am vexed to see it.
  Late hours and wine, Castiglione, – these
  Will ruin thee! thou art already altered –
  Thy looks are haggard – nothing so wears away
  The constitution as late hours and wine.
CAS.  (*musing*) Nothing, fair cousin, nothing – not even deep
    sorrow –
  Wears it away like evil hours and wine.
  I will amend.
ALESS.            Do it! I would have thee drop

Thy riotous company, too – fellows low born –
Ill suit the like with old Di Broglio's heir
And Alessandra's husband.

CAS.                I will drop them.

ALESS.   Thou wilt – thou must. Attend thou also more
To thy dress and equipage – they are over plain
For thy lofty rank and fashion – much depends
Upon appearances.

CAS.             I'll see to it.

ALESS.   Then see to it! – pay more attention, sir,
To a becoming carriage – much thou wantest
In dignity.

CAS.        Much, much, oh much I want
In proper dignity.

ALESS.   (*haughtily*) Thou mockest me, sir!

CAS.   (*abstractedly*) Sweet, gentle Lalage!

ALESS.               Heard I aright?
I speak to him – he speaks of Lalage!
Sir Count! (*places her hand on his shoulder*) what art thou
    dreaming? he's not well!
What ails thee, sir?

CAS.   (*starting*) Cousin! fair cousin! – madam!
I crave thy pardon – indeed I am not well –
Your hand from off my shoulder, if you please.
This air is most oppressive! – Madam – the Duke!

Enter DI BROGLIO

DI BROGLIO.   My son, I've news for thee! – hey? – what's the
    matter? (*observing Alessandra*)
I' the pouts? Kiss her, Castiglione! kiss her,
You dog! and make it up, I say, this minute!
I've news for you both. Politian is expected
Hourly in Rome – Politian, Earl of Leicester!
We'll have him at the wedding. 'Tis his first visit
To the imperial city.

ALESS.          What! Politian
Of Britain, Earl of Leicester?

DI BROG.           The same, my love.
We'll have him at the wedding. A man quite young

In years, but grey in fame. I have not seen him,
But Rumour speaks of him as of a prodigy
Pre-eminent in arts and arms, and wealth,
And high descent. We'll have him at the wedding.

ALESS. I have heard much of this Politian.
Gay, volatile and giddy – is he not?
And little given to thinking.

DI BROG.                          Far from it, love.
No branch, they say, of all philosophy
So deep abstruse he has not mastered it.
Learned as few are learned.

ALESS.                          'Tis very strange!
I have known men have seen Politian
And sought his company. They speak of him
As of one who entered madly into life,
Drinking the cup of pleasure to the dregs.

CAS. Ridiculous! Now *I* have seen Politian
And know him well – nor learned nor mirthful he.
He is a dreamer and a man shut out
From common passions.

DI BROG.                    Children, we disagree.
Let us go forth and taste the fragrant air
Of the garden. Did I dream, or did I hear
Politian was a *melancholy* man?                    (*Exeunt*)


2


*A Lady's apartment, with a window open and looking into a garden.*
LALAGE, *in deep mourning, reading at a table on which lie some books
and a hand mirror. In the background* JACINTA (*a servant maid*) *leans
carelessly upon a chair.*

LAL.  Jacinta! is it thou?
JAC.  (*pertly*)                Yes, Ma'am, I'm here.
LAL.  I did not know, Jacinta, you were in waiting.
Sit down! – let not my presence trouble you –

Sit down! – for I am humble, most humble.

JAC. (*aside*)                                    'Tis time.

JACINTA *seats herself in a side-long manner upon the chair, resting her elbows upon the back, and regarding her mistress with a contemptuous look.* LALAGE *continues to read.*

LAL.  'It in another climate, so he said,
    Bore a bright golden flower, but not i' this soil?'

        (*pauses – turns over some leaves, and resumes*)

    'No lingering winters there, nor snow, nor shower –
    But Ocean ever to refresh mankind
    Breathes the shrill spirit of the western wind.'
    Oh, beautiful! – most beautiful! – how like
    To what my fevered soul doth dream of Heaven!
    O happy land! (*pauses*) She died! – the maiden died!
    O still more happy maiden who couldst die!
    Jacinta!

JACINTA *returns no answer, and* LALAGE *presently resumes.*

    Again! – a similar tale
    Told of a beauteous dame beyond the sea!
    Thus speaketh one Ferdinand in the words of the play –
    'She died full young' – one Bossola answers him –
    'I think not so – her infelicity
    Seemed to have years too many' – Ah luckless lady!
    Jacinta! (*still no answer*)
    Here's a far sterner story
    But like – oh, very like in its despair –
    Of that Egyptian queen, winning so easily
    A thousand hearts – losing at length her own.
    She died. Thus endeth the history – and her maids
    Lean over her and weep – two gentle maids
    With gentle names – Eiros and Charmion?
    Rainbow and Dove! – Jacinta!

JAC.  (*pettishly*)                    Madam, what *is* it?

LAL.  Wilt thou, my good Jacinta, be so kind
    As go down in the library and bring me
    The Holy Evangelists.

JAC.                    Pshaw!                    (*Exit*)

LAL.                              If there be balm
  For the wounded spirit in Gilead it is there!
  Dew in the night time of my bitter trouble
  Will there be found – 'dew sweeter far than that
  Which hangs like chains of pearl on Hermon Hill.'

*Re-enter* JACINTA, *and throws a volume on the table.*

  There, ma'am,'s the book. Indeed she is very troublesome.
(*aside*)
LAL. (*astonished*) What didst thou say, Jacinta? Have I done
    aught
  To grieve thee or to vex thee? – I am sorry.
  For thou hast served me long and ever been
  Trust-worthy and respectful. (*resumes her reading*)
JAC.                              I can't believe
  She has any more jewels – no – no – she gave me all. (*aside*)
LAL.  What didst thou say, Jacinta? Now I bethink me
  Thou hast not spoken lately of thy wedding.
  How fares good Ugo? – and when is it to be?
  Can I do aught? – is there no farther aid
  Thou needest, Jacinta?
JAC.                              Is there no *farther* aid!
  That's meant for me. (*aside*) I'm sure, Madam, you need not
  Be always throwing those jewels in my teeth.
LAL.  Jewels! Jacinta, – now indeed, Jacinta,
  I thought not of the jewels.
JAC.                              Oh! perhaps not!
  But then I might have sworn it. After all,
  There's Ugo says the ring is only paste,
  For he's sure the Count Castiglione never
  Would have given a real diamond to such as you;
  And at the best I'm certain, Madam, you cannot
  Have use for jewels *now*. But I might have sworn it.          (*Exit*)

LALAGE *bursts into tears and leans her head upon the table – after a
short pause raises it.*

LAL.  Poor Lalage! – and is it come to this?
  Thy servant maid! – but courage! – 'tis but a viper
  Whom thou hast cherished to sting thee to the soul!

(*taking up the mirror*)

Ha! here at least's a friend – too much a friend
In earlier days – a friend will not deceive thee.
Fair mirror and true! now tell me (for thou canst)
A tale – a pretty tale – and heed thou not
Though it be rife with woe. It answers me.
It speaks of sunken eyes, and wasted cheeks,
And Beauty long deceased – remembers me
Of Joy departed – Hope, the Seraph Hope,
Inurned and entombed! – now, in a tone
Low, sad, and solemn, but most audible,
Whispers of early grave untimely yawning
For ruined maid. Fair mirror and true! – thou liest not!
*Thou* hast no end to gain – no heart to break –
Castiglione lied who said he loved –
Thou true – he false! – false! – false!

*While she speaks, a* MONK *enters her apartment, and approaches*
*unobserved.*

MONK.                                    Refuge thou hast,
    Sweet daughter! in Heaven. Think of eternal things!
    Give up thy soul to penitence, and pray!
LAL.  (*arising hurriedly*) I *cannot* pray! – My soul is at war with
        God!
    The frightful sounds of merriment below
    Disturb my senses – go! I cannot pray –
    The sweet airs from the garden worry me!
    Thy presence grieves me – go! – thy priestly raiment
    Fills me with dread – thy ebony crucifix
    With horror and awe!
MONK.                    Think of thy precious soul!
LAL.  Think of my early days! – think of my father
    And mother in Heaven! think of our quiet home,
    And the rivulet that ran before the door!
    Think of my little sisters – think of them!
    And think of me! – think of my trusting love
    And confidence – his vows – my ruin – think – think
    Of my unspeakable misery! – begone!
    Yet stay! yet stay! – what was it thou saidst of prayer
    And penitence? Didst thou not speak of faith

And vows before the throne?

MONK.                                    I did.

LAL.                                    'Tis well.
  There *is* a vow were fitting should be made –
  A sacred vow, imperative, and urgent,
  A solemn vow!

MONK.  Daughter, this zeal is well!

LAL.  Father, this zeal is anything but well!
  Hast thou a crucifix fit for this thing?
  A crucifix whereon to register
  This sacred vow? (*He hands her his own.*)

LAL.              Not that – Oh! no! – no! – no!      (*shuddering*)
  Not that! Not that! – I tell thee, holy man
  Thy raiments and thy ebony cross affright me!
  Stand back! I have a crucifix myself,–
  *I* have a crucifix! Methinks 'twere fitting
  The deed – the vow – the symbol of the deed –
  And the deed's register should tally, father!

       (*draws a cross-handled dagger and raises it on high*)

  Behold the cross wherewith a vow like mine
  Is written in Heaven!

MONK.                   Thy words are madness, daughter,
  And speak a purpose unholy – thy lips are livid –
  Thine eyes are wild – tempt not the wrath divine!
  Pause ere too late! – oh be not – be not rash!
  Swear not the oath – oh swear it not.

LAL.                                    'Tis sworn!


                              3

*An apartment in a palace.* POLITIAN *and* BALDAZZAR.

BALDAZZAR.  – Arouse thee now, Politian!
  Thou must not – nay indeed, indeed, thou shalt not
  Give way unto these humours. Be thyself!
  Shake off the idle fancies that beset thee,
  And live, for now thou diest!

POLITIAN.                        Not so, Baldazzar!
  *Surely* I live.

BAL.  Politian, it doth grieve me

To see thee thus.

POL.  Baldazzar, it doth grieve me
To give thee cause for grief, my honoured friend.
Command me, sir! what wouldst thou have me do?
At thy behest I will shake off that nature
Which from my forefathers I did inherit,
Which with my mother's milk I did imbibe,
And be no more Politian, but some other.
Command me, sir!

BAL.                To the field then – to the field –
To the senate or the field.

POL.                Alas! alas!
There is an imp would follow me even there!
There is an imp *hath* followed me even there!
There is – what voice was that?

BAL.                I heard it not.
I heard not any voice except thine own,
And the echo of thine own.

POL.                Then I but dreamed.

BAL.  Give not thy soul to dreams: the camp – the court
Befit thee – Fame awaits thee – Glory calls –
And her the trumpet-tongued thou wilt not hear
In hearkening to imaginary sounds
And phantom voices.

POL.                It *is* a phantom voice!
Didst thou not hear it *then*?

BAL.                I heard it not.

POL.  Thou heardst it not! – Baldazzar, speak no more
To me, Politian, of thy camps and courts.
Oh! I am sick, sick, sick, even unto death,
Of the hollow and high-sounding vanities
Of the populous Earth! Bear with me yet awhile!
We have been boys together – school-fellows –
And now are friends – yet shall not be so long –
For in the eternal city thou shalt do me
A kind and gentle office, and a Power –
A Power august, benignant and supreme –
Shall then absolve thee of all farther duties
Unto thy friend.

BAL.             Thou speakest a fearful riddle

I *will* not understand.

POL.                     Yet now as Fate
  Approaches, and the Hours are breathing low,
  The sands of Time are changed to golden grains,
  And dazzle me, Baldazzar. Alas! alas!
  I *cannot* die, having within my heart
  So keen a relish for the beautiful
  As hath been kindled within it. Methinks the air
  Is balmier now than it was wont to be —
  Rich melodies are floating in the winds —
  A rarer loveliness bedecks the earth —
  And with a holier lustre the quiet moon
  Sitteth in Heaven. — Hist! hist! thou canst not say
  Thou hearest not *now*, Baldazzar?

BAL.  Indeed I hear not.

POL.  Not hear it! — listen now — listen! — the faintest sound
  And yet the sweetest that ear ever heard!
  A lady's voice! — and sorrow in the tone!
  Baldazzar, it oppresses me like a spell!
  Again! — again! — how solemnly it falls
  Into my heart of hearts! that eloquent voice
  Surely I never heard — yet it were well
  Had I *but* heard it with its thrilling tones
  In earlier days!

BAL.            I myself hear it now.
  Be still! — the voice, if I mistake not greatly,
  Proceeds from yonder lattice — which you may see
  Very plainly through the window — it belongs,
  Does it not? unto this palace of the Duke.
  The singer is undoubtedly beneath
  The roof of his Excellency — and perhaps
  Is even that Alessandra of whom he spoke
  As the betrothed of Castiglione,
  His son and heir.

POL.  Be still! — it comes again!

VOICE  (*very faintly*) 'And is thy heart so strong
                        As for to leave me thus
                        Who hath loved thee so long
                        In wealth and wo among?
                        And is thy heart so strong

As for to leave me thus?
>Say nay – say nay!'

BAL. The song is English, and I oft have heard it
In merry England – never so plaintively –
Hist! hist! it comes again!

VOICE (*more loudly*)     'Is it so strong
As for to leave me thus
Who hath loved thee so long
In wealth and wo among?
And is thy heart so strong
As for to leave me thus?
>Say nay – say nay!'

BAL. 'Tis hushed and all is still!

POL.                 All *is not* still.

BAL. Let us go down.

POL.            Go down, Baldazzar, go!

BAL. The hour is growing late – the Duke awaits us, –
Thy presence is expected in the hall
Below. What ails thee, Earl Politian?

VOICE (*distinctly*)     'Who hath loved thee so long,
In wealth and wo among,
And is thy heart so strong?
>Say nay – say nay!'

BAL. Let us descend! – 'tis time. Politian, give
These fancies to the wind. Remember, pray,
Your bearing lately savoured much of rudeness
Unto the Duke. Arouse thee! and remember!

POL. Remember? I do. Lead on! I *do* remember.(*going*)
Let us descend. Believe me I would give,
Freely would give the broad lands of my earldom
To look upon the face hidden by yon lattice –
'To gaze upon that veiled face, and hear
Once more that silent tongue.'

BAL.               Let me beg you, sir.
Descend with me – the Duke may be offended.
Let us go down, I pray you.

VOICE (*loudly*) Say nay! – say nay!

POL. (*aside*) 'Tis strange – 'tis very strange – methought the voice
Chimed in with my desires and bade me stay!

(*approaching the window*)

Sweet voice! I heed thee, and will surely stay.
Now be this Fancy, by Heaven, or be it Fate,
Still will I not descend. Baldazzar, make
Apology unto the Duke for me;
I go not down to-night.

BAL.                    Your lordship's pleasure
Shall be attended to. Good night, Politian.

POL.  Good night, my friend, good night.


4

*The gardens of a palace – Moonlight.* LALAGE *and* POLITIAN.

LALAGE.  And dost thou speak of love
To *me*, Politian? – dost thou speak of love
To Lalage? – ah wo – ah wo is me!
This mockery is most cruel – most cruel indeed!

POLITIAN.  Weep not! oh, sob not thus! – thy bitter tears
Will madden me. Oh mourn not, Lalage –
Be comforted! I know – I know it all,
And *still* I speak of love. Look at me, brightest,
And beautiful Lalage! – turn here thine eyes!
Thou askest me if I could speak of love,
Knowing what I know, and seeing what I have seen.
Thou askest me that – and thus I answer thee –
Thus on my bended knee I answer thee. (*kneeling*)
Sweet Lalage, *I love thee – love thee – love thee*;
Thro' good and ill – thro' weal and wo *I love thee.*
Not mother, with her first born on her knee,
Thrills with intenser love than I for thee.
Not on God's altar, in any time or clime,
Burned there a holier fire than burneth now
Within my spirit for *thee.* And do I love? (*arising*)
Even for thy woes I love thee – even for thy woes –
Thy beauty and thy woes.

LAL.                    Alas, proud Earl,
Thou dost forget thyself, remembering me!
How, in thy father's halls, among the maidens
Pure and reproachless of thy princely line,
Could the dishonoured Lalage abide?

Thy wife, and with a tainted memory –
My seared and blighted name, how would it tally
With the ancestral honours of thy house,
And with thy glory?
POL.                    Speak not to me of glory!
  I hate – I loathe the name; I do abhor
  The unsatisfactory and ideal thing.
  Art thou not Lalage and I Politian?
  Do I not love – art thou not beautiful –
  What need we more? Ha! glory! – now speak not of it:
  By all I hold most sacred and most solemn –
  By all my wishes now – my fears hereafter –
  By all I scorn on earth and hope in heaven –
  There is no deed I would more glory in,
  Than in thy cause to scoff at this same glory
  And trample it under foot. What matters it –
  What matters it, my fairest, and my best,
  That we go down unhonoured and forgotten
  Into the dust – so we descend together.
  Descend together – and then – and then perchance –
LAL.  Why dost thou pause, Politian?
POL.                              And then perchance
  *Arise* together, Lalage, and roam
  The starry and quiet dwellings of the blest,
  And still –
LAL.        Why dost thou pause, Politian?
POL.  And still *together – together.*
LAL.                          Now Earl of Leicester!
  Thou *lovest* me, and in my heart of hearts
  I feel thou lovest me truly.
POL.  Oh, Lalage! (*throwing himself upon his knee*)
  And lovest thou *me*?
LAL.                  Hist! hush! within the gloom
  Of yonder trees methought a figure past –
  A spectral figure, solemn, and slow, and noiseless –
  Like the grim shadow Conscience, solemn and noiseless.

                    (*walks across and returns*)

  I was mistaken – 'twas but a giant bough
  Stirred by the autumn wind. Politian!

POL.   My Lalage – my love! why art thou moved?
   Why dost thou turn so pale? Not Conscience' self,
   Far less a shadow which thou likenest to it,
   Should shake the firm spirit thus. But the night wind
   Is chilly – and these melancholy boughs
   Throw over all things a gloom.

LAL.                              Politian!
   Thou speakest to me of love. Knowest thou the land
   With which all tongues are busy – a land new found –
   Miraculously found by one of Genoa –
   A thousand leagues within the golden west?
   A fairy land of flowers, and fruit, and sunshine,
   And crystal lakes, and over-arching forests,
   And mountains, around whose towering summits the winds
   Of Heaven untrammelled flow – which air to breathe
   Is Happiness now, and will be Freedom hereafter
   In days that are to come?

POL.   O, wilt thou – wilt thou
   Fly to that Paradise – my Lalage, wilt thou
   Fly thither with me? There Care shall be forgotten
   And Sorrow shall be no more, and Eros be all.
   And life shall then be mine, for I will live
   For thee, and in thine eyes – and thou shalt be
   No more a mourner – but the radiant Joys
   Shall wait upon thee, and the angel Hope
   Attend thee ever; and I will kneel to thee
   And worship thee, and call thee my beloved,
   My own, my beautiful, my love, my wife,
   My all – oh, wilt thou – wilt thou, Lalage,
   Fly thither with me?

LAL.                     A deed is to be done –
   Castiglione lives!

POL.              And he shall die!                    (*Exit*)

LAL.   (*after a pause*) – And – he – shall – die! – alas!
   Castiglione die? Who spoke the words?
   Where am I? – what was it he said? – Politian!
   Thou *art* not gone – thou art not *gone*, Politian!
   I *feel* thou art not gone – yet dare not look,
   Lest I behold thee not; thou *couldst* not go
   With those words upon thy lips – O, speak to me!

And let me hear thy voice – one word – one word,
To say thou art not gone, – one little sentence,
To say how thou dost scorn – how thou dost hate
My womanly weakness. Ha! ha! thou *art* not gone –
O speak to me! I *knew* thou wouldst not go!
I knew thou wouldst not, couldst not, *durst* not go.
Villain, thou *art* not gone – thou mockest me!
And thus I clutch thee – thus! – He is gone, he is gone –
Gone – gone. Where am I? – 'tis well – 'tis very well!
So that the blade be keen – the blow be sure,
'Tis well, 'tis *very* well – alas! alas!                    (*Exit*)

5

*The suburbs.* POLITIAN *alone.*

POLITIAN.  This weakness grows upon me. I am faint,
    And much I fear me ill – it will not do
    To die ere I have lived! Stay – stay thy hand,
    O Azrael, yet awhile! – Prince of the Powers
    Of Darkness and the Tomb, O pity me!
    O pity me! let me not perish now,
    In the budding of my Paradisal Hope!
    Give me to live yet – yet a little while:
    'Tis I who pray for life – I who so late
    Demanded but to die! – what sayeth the Count?

Enter BALDAZZAR

BALDAZZAR.  That knowing no cause of quarrel or of feud
    Between the Earl Politian and himself,
    He doth decline your cartel.
POL.  *What* didst thou say?
    What answer was it you brought me, good Baldazzar?
    With what excessive fragrance the zephyr comes
    Laden from yonder bowers! – a fairer day,
    Or one more worthy Italy, methinks
    No mortal eyes have seen! – *what* said the Count?
BAL.  That he, Castiglione, not being aware
    Of any feud existing, or any cause
    Of quarrel between your lordship and himself
    Cannot accept the challenge.

POL. It is most true –
    All this is very true. When saw you, sir,
    When saw you now, Baldazzar, in the frigid
    Ungenial Britain which we left so lately,
    A heaven so calm as this – so utterly free
    From the evil taint of clouds? – and he did *say?*
BAL. No more, my lord, than I have told you, sir:
    The Count Castiglione will not fight,
    Having no cause for quarrel.
POL. Now this is true –
    All very true. Thou art my friend, Baldazzar,
    And I have not forgotten it – thou'lt do me
    A piece of service; wilt thou go back and say
    Unto this man, that I, the Earl of Leicester,
    Hold him a villain? – thus much, I prythee, say
    Unto the Count – it is exceeding just
    He should have cause for quarrel.
BAL.               My lord! – my friend! –
POL. (*aside*) 'Tis he – he comes himself! (*aloud*) thou reasonest well.
    I know what thou wouldst say – not send the message –
    Well! – I will think of it – I will not send it.
    Now prythee, leave me – hither doth come a person
    With whom affairs of a most private nature
    I would adjust.
BAL.             I go – to-morrow we meet.
    Do we not? – at the Vatican.
POL. At the Vatican.                  (*Exit* BAL.)

Enter CASTIGLIONE

CAS. The Earl of Leicester here!
POL. I *am* the Earl of Leicester, and thou seest,
    Dost thou not? that I am here.
CAS.               My lord, some strange,
    Some singular mistake – misunderstanding –
    Hath without doubt arisen: thou hast been urged
    Thereby, in heat of anger, to address
    Some words most unaccountable, in writing,
    To me, Castiglione; the bearer being

Baldazzar, Duke of Surrey. I am aware
Of nothing which might warrant thee in this thing,
Having given thee no offence. Ha! – am I right?
'Twas a mistake? – undoubtedly – we all
Do err at times.

POL. Draw, villain, and prate no more!

CAS. Ha! – draw? – and villain? have at thee then at once,–
Proud Earl! (*draws*)

POL. (*drawing*) Thus to the expiatory tomb,
Untimely sepulchre, I do devote thee
In the name of Lalage!

CAS. (*letting fall his sword and recoiling to the extremity of the stage*)
Of Lalage!
Hold off – thy sacred hand! – avaunt I say!
Avaunt – I will not fight thee – indeed I dare not.

POL. Thou wilt not fight with me didst say, Sir Count?
Shall I be baffled thus? – now this is well;
Didst say thou *darest* not? Ha!

CAS. I dare not – dare not –
Hold off thy hand – with that beloved name
So fresh upon thy lips I will not fight thee –
I cannot – dare not.

POL. Now by my halidom
I do believe thee! – coward, I do believe thee!

CAS. Ha! – coward! – this may not be!

(*clutches his sword and staggers towards* POLITIAN, *but his purpose is changed before reaching him, and he falls upon his knee at the feet of the Earl*)

Alas! my lord,
It is – it is – most true. In such a cause
I am the veriest coward. O pity me!

POL. (*greatly softened*) Alas! – I do – indeed I pity thee.

CAS. And Lalage –

POL. *Scoundrel! – arise and die!*

CAS. It needeth not be – thus – thus – O let me die
Thus on my bended knee. It were most fitting
That in this deep humiliation I perish.
For in the fight I will not raise a hand

Against thee, Earl of Leicester. Strike thou home –
                 (*baring his bosom*)
Here is no let or hindrance to thy weapon –
Strike home. I *will not* fight thee.

POL.                           Now's Death and Hell!
Am I not – am I not sorely – grievously tempted
To take thee at thy word? But mark me, sir:
Think not to fly me thus. Do thou prepare
For public insult in the streets – before
The eyes of the citizens. I'll follow thee –
Like an avenging spirit I'll follow thee
Even unto death. Before those whom thou lovest –
Before all Rome I'll taunt thee, villain, – I'll taunt thee,
Dost hear? with *cowardice* – thou *wilt not* fight me?
Thou liest! thou *shalt*!                            (*Exit*)

CAS.                    Now this indeed is just!
Most righteous, and most just, avenging Heaven!


# Bridal Ballad


TO —

The ring is on my hand,
   And the wreath is on my brow;
Satins and jewels grand
Are all at my command,
   And I am happy now.


And my lord he loves me well;
   But, when first he breathed his vow,
I felt my bosom swell –
For the words rang as a knell,
And the voice seemed *his* who fell
In the battle down the dell,
   And who is happy now.

But he spoke to re-assure me,
    And he kissed my pallid brow,
While a reverie came o'er me,
And to the churchyard bore me,
And I sighed to him before me,
(Thinking him dead D'Elormie),
    'Oh, I am happy now!'

And thus the words were spoken;
    And this the plighted vow;
And, though my faith be broken,
And, though my heart be broken,
Here is a ring as token
    That I am happy now!

Would God I could awaken!
    For I dream I know not how,
And my soul is sorely shaken
Lest an evil step be taken,–
Lest the dead who is forsaken
    May not be happy now.

## Sonnet to Zante

Fair isle, that from the fairest of all flowers,
    Thy gentlest of all gentle names dost take!
How many memories of what radiant hours
    At sight of thee and thine at once awake!
How many scenes of what departed bliss!
    How many thoughts of what entombéd hopes!
How many visions of a maiden that is
    No more – no more upon thy verdant slopes!
No *more!* alas,that magical sad sound
    Transforming all! Thy charms shall please *no more* –
Thy memory *no more!* Accurséd ground
    Henceforth I hold thy flower-enamelled shore,

O hyacinthine isle! O purple Zante!
'Isola d'oro! Fior di Levante!'


# The Haunted Palace


In the greenest of our valleys
    By good angels tenanted,
Once a fair and stately palace –
    Radiant palace – reared its head.
In the monarch Thought's dominion –
    It stood there!
Never seraph spread a pinion
    Over fabric half so fair!

Banners yellow, glorious, golden,
    On its roof did float and flow,
(This – all this – was in the olden
    Time long ago,)
And every gentle air that dallied,
    In that sweet day,
Along the ramparts plumed and pallid,
    A wingéd odour went away.

Wanderers in that happy valley,
    Through two luminous windows, saw
Spirits moving musically,
    To a lute's well-tunéd law,
Round about a throne where, sitting,
    (Porphyrogene!)
In state his glory well befitting,
    The ruler of the realm was seen.

And all with pearl and ruby glowing
    Was the fair palace door,
Through which came flowing, flowing, flowing
    And sparkling evermore,

A troop of Echoes, whose sweet duty
   Was but to sing,
In voices of surpassing beauty,
   The wit and wisdom of their king.

But evil things, in robes of sorrow,
   Assailed the monarch's high estate.
(Ah, let us mourn! – for never morrow
   Shall dawn upon him desolate!)
And round about his home the glory
   That blushed and bloomed,
Is but a dim-remembered story
   Of the old time entombed.

And travellers, now, within that valley,
   Through the red-litten windows see
Vast forms, that move fantastically
   To a discordant melody,
While, like a ghastly rapid river,
   Through the pale door
A hideous throng rush out forever
   And laugh – but smile no more.

# Sonnet – Silence

There are some qualities – some incorporate things,
   That have a double life, which thus is made
A type of that twin entity which springs
   From matter and light, evinced in solid and shade.
There is a two-fold *Silence* – sea and shore –
   Body and soul. One dwells in lonely places,
   Newly with grass o'ergrown; some solemn graces,
Some human memories and tearful lore,
Render him terrorless: his name's 'No More'.
He is the corporate Silence: dread him not!
   No power hath he of evil in himself;

But should some urgent fate (untimely lot!)
   Bring thee to meet his shadow (nameless elf,
That haunteth the lone regions where hath trod
No foot of man,) commend thyself to God!

# The Conqueror Worm

Lo! 'tis a gala night
   Within the lonesome latter years!
An angel throng, bewinged, bedight
   In veins, and drowned in tears,
Sit in a theatre, to see
   A play of hopes and fears,
While the orchestra breathes fitfully
   The music of the spheres.

Mimes, in the form of God on high,
   Mutter and mumble low,
And hither and thither fly –
   Mere puppets they, who come and go
At bidding of vast formless things
   That shift the scenery to and fro,
Flapping from out their Condor wings
   Invisible Wo!

That motley drama – oh, be sure
   It shall not be forgot!
With its Phantom chased for evermore.
   By a crowd that seize it not,
Through a circle that ever returneth in
   To the self-same spot,
And much of Madness, and more of Sin,
   And Horror the soul of the plot.

But see, amid the mimic rout
   A crawling shape intrude!

A blood-red thing that writhes from out
  The scenic solitude!
It writhes! – it writhes! – with mortal pangs
  The mimes become its food,
And seraphs sob at vermin fangs
  In human gore imbued.

Out – out are the lights – out all!
  And, over each quivering form,
The curtain, a funeral pall,
  Comes down with the rush of a storm,
While the angels, all pallid and wan,
  Uprising, unveiling, affirm
That the play is the tragedy, 'Man',
  And its hero the Conqueror Worm.

# Dream-Land

By a route obscure and lonely,
Haunted by ill angels only,
Where an Eidolon, named NIGHT,
On a black throne reigns upright,
I have reached these lands but newly
  From an ultimate dim Thule –
From a wild weird clime that lieth, sublime,
  Out of SPACE – out of TIME.

Bottomless vales and boundless floods,
And chasms, and caves and Titan woods,
With forms that no man can discover
For the tears that drip all over;
Mountains toppling evermore
Into seas without a shore;
Seas that restlessly aspire,
Surging, unto skies of fire;
Lakes that endlessly outspread

Their lone waters – lone and dead, –
Their still waters – still and chilly
With the snows of the lolling lily.

By the lakes that thus outspread
Their lone waters, lone and dead, –
Their sad waters, sad and chilly
With the snows of the lolling lily, –
By the mountains – near the river
Murmuring lowly, murmuring ever, –
By the grey woods, – by the swamp
Where the toad and the newt encamp, –
By the dismal tarns and pools
  Where dwell the Ghouls, –
By each spot the most unholy –
In each nook most melancholy, –
There the traveller meets, aghast,
Sheeted Memories of the Past –
Shrouded forms that start and sigh
As they pass the wanderer by –
White-robed forms of friends long given,
In agony, to the Earth – and Heaven.

For the heart whose woes are legion
'Tis a peaceful, soothing region –
For the spirit that walks in shadow
'Tis – oh 'tis an Eldorado!
But the traveller, travelling through it,
May not – dare not openly view it;
Never its mysteries are exposed
To the weak human eye unclosed;
So wills its King, who hath forbid
The uplifting of the fringéd lid;
And thus the sad Soul that here passes
Beholds it but through darkened glasses.

By a route obscure and lonely,
Haunted by ill angels only,
Where an Eidolon, named NIGHT,
On a black throne reigns upright,

I have wandered home but newly
From this ultimate dim Thule.

# The Raven

Once upon a midnight dreary, while I pondered, weak and
        weary,
Over many a quaint and curious volume of forgotten lore –
While I nodded, nearly napping, suddenly there came a
        tapping,
As of some one gently rapping, rapping at my chamber door.
''Tis some visiter,' I muttered, 'tapping at my chamber door –
                Only this and nothing more.'

Ah, distinctly I remember it was in the bleak December;
And each separate dying ember wrought its ghost upon the
        floor.
Eagerly I wished the morrow; – vainly I had sought to borrow
From my books surcease of sorrow – sorrow for the lost
        Lenore –
For the rare and radiant maiden whom the angels name
        Lenore –
                Nameless *here* for evermore.

And the silken, sad, uncertain rustling of each purple curtain
Thrilled me – filled me with fantastic terrors never felt before;
So that now, to still the beating of my heart, I stood repeating
''Tis some visiter entreating entrance at my chamber door –
Some late visiter entreating entrance at my chamber door; –
                This it is and nothing more.'

Presently my soul grew stronger; hesitating then no longer,
'Sir,' said I, 'or Madam, truly your forgiveness I implore;
But the fact is I was napping, and so gently you came rapping,
And so faintly you came tapping, tapping at my chamber door,

That I scarce was sure I heard you' – here I opened wide the
     door; –
                    Darkness there and nothing more.

Deep into that darkness peering, long I stood there wondering,
     fearing,
Doubting, dreaming dreams no mortal ever dared to dream
     before;
But the silence was unbroken, and the stillness gave no token,
And the only word there spoken was the whispered word,
     'Lenore!'
This I whispered, and an echo murmured back the word
     'Lenore!'
                    Merely this and nothing more.

Back into the chamber turning, all my soul within me
     burning,
Soon again I heard a tapping somewhat louder than before
'Surely,' said I, 'surely that is something at my window lattice;
Let me see, then, what thereat is, and this mystery explore –
Let my heart be still a moment and this mystery explore; –
                    'Tis the wind and nothing more!'

Open here I flung the shutter, when, with many a flirt and
     flutter
In there stepped a stately Raven of the saintly days of yore.
Not the least obeisance made he; not a minute stopped or
     stayed he;
But, with mien of lord or lady, perched above my chamber
     door –
Perched upon a bust of Pallas just above my chamber door –
                    Perched, and sat, and nothing more.

Then this ebony bird beguiling my sad fancy into smiling,
By the grave and stern decorum of the countenance it wore,
'Though thy crest be shorn and shaven, thou,' I said, 'art sure
     no craven,
Ghastly grim and ancient Raven wandering from the Nightly
     shore –
Tell me what thy lordly name is on the Night's Plutonian
     shore!'
                    Quoth the Raven, 'Nevermore.'

Much I marvelled this ungainly fowl to hear discourse so plainly,
Though its answer little meaning – little relevancy bore;
For we cannot help agreeing that no living human being
Ever yet was blessed with seeing bird above his chamber
    door –
Bird or beast upon the sculptured bust above his chamber
    door,
               With such name as 'Nevermore.'

But the Raven, sitting lonely on the placid bust, spoke only
That one word, as if his soul in that one word he did outpour.
Nothing farther then he uttered – not a feather then he
    fluttered –
Till I scarcely more than muttered 'Other friends have flown
    before –
On the morrow *he* will leave me, as my hopes have flown
    before.'
               Then the bird said 'Nevermore.'

Startled at the stillness broken by reply so aptly spoken,
'Doubtless,' said I, 'what it utters is its only stock and store
Caught from some unhappy master whom unmerciful Disaster
Followed fast and followed faster till his songs one burden
    bore –
Till the dirges of his Hope that melancholy burden bore
               Of "Never – nevermore." '

But the Raven still beguiling all my fancy into smiling,
Straight I wheeled a cushioned seat in front of bird, and bust
    and door;
Then, upon the velvet sinking, I betook myself to linking
Fancy unto fancy, thinking what this ominous bird of yore –
What this grim, ungainly, ghastly, gaunt, and ominous bird of
    yore
               Meant in croaking 'Nevermore.'

This I sat engaged in guessing, but no syllable expressing
To the fowl whose fiery eyes now burned into my bosom's
    core;

This and more I sat divining, with my head at ease reclining
On the cushion's velvet lining that the lamp-light gloated o'er,
But whose velvet violet lining with the lamp-light gloating
    o'er,
              *She* shall press, ah, nevermore!

Then, methought, the air grew denser, perfumed from an
    unseen censer
Swung by Seraphim whose foot-falls tinkled on the tufted
    floor.
'Wretch,' I cried, 'thy God hath lent thee – by these angels he
    hath sent thee
Respite – respite and nepenthe from thy memories of Lenore;
Quaff, oh quaff this kind nepenthe and forget this lost Lenore!'
           Quoth the Raven 'Nevermore.'

'Prophet!' said I, 'thing of evil! prophet still, if bird or devil! –
Whether Tempter sent, or whether tempest tossed thee here
    ashore,
Desolate yet all undaunted, on this desert land enchanted –
On this home by Horror haunted – tell me truly, I implore –
Is there – *is* there balm in Gilead? – tell me – tell me, I implore!'
           Quoth the Raven 'Nevermore.'

'Prophet!' said I, 'thing of evil! – prophet still, if bird or devil!
By that Heaven that bends above us – by that God we both
    adore –
Tell this soul with sorrow laden if, within the distant Aidenn,
It shall clasp a sainted maiden whom the angels name
    Lenore –
Clasp a rare and radiant maiden whom the angels name
    Lenore.'
           Quoth the Raven 'Nevermore.'

'Be that word our sign of parting, bird or fiend!' I shrieked,
    upstarting –
'Get thee back into the tempest and the Night's Plutonian
    shore!
Leave no black plume as a token of that lie thy soul hath
    spoken!

Leave my loneliness unbroken! – quit the bust above my door!
Take thy beak from out my heart, and take thy form from off
    my door!'
              Quoth the Raven 'Nevermore.'

And the Raven, never flitting, still is sitting, *still* is sitting
On the pallid bust of Pallas just above my chamber door;
And his eyes have all the seeming of a demon's that is
    dreaming,
And the lamp-light o'er him streaming throws his shadow on
    the floor;
And my soul from out that shadow that lies floating on the
    floor
              Shall be lifted – nevermore!

## Eulalie – a Song

            I dwelt alone
            In a world of moan,
        And my soul was a stagnant tide,

Till the fair and gentle Eulalie became my blushing bride –
Till the yellow-haired young Eulalie became my smiling bride.

            Ah, less – less bright
            The stars of the night
        Than the eyes of the radiant girl!
            And never a flake
            That the vapour can make
        With the moon-tints of purple and pearl,
Can vie with the modest Eulalie's most unregarded curl –
Can compare with the bright-eyed Eulalie's most humble and
    careless curl.

Now Doubt – now Pain
Come never again,
For her soul gives me sigh for sigh,
And all day long
Shines, bright and strong,
Astarté within the sky,
While ever to her dear Eulalie upturns her matron eye –
While ever to her young Eulalie upturns her violet eye.

# A Valentine

TO — — —

For her this rhyme is penned, whose luminous eyes,
  Brightly expressive as the twins of Leda,
Shall find her own sweet name, that, nestling lies
  Upon the page, enwrapped from every reader,
Search narrowly the lines! – they hold a treasure
  Divine – a talisman – an amulet
That must be worn *at heart*. Search well the measure –
  The words – the syllables! Do not forget
The trivialest point, or you may lose your labour!
  And yet there is in this no Gordian knot
Which one might not undo without a sabre,
  If one could merely comprehend the plot.
Enwritten upon the leaf where now are peering
  Eyes scintillating soul, there lie *perdus*
Three eloquent words oft uttered in the hearing
  Of poets, by poets – as the name is a poet's, too,
Its letters, although naturally lying
  Like the knight Pinto – Mendez Ferdinando –
Still form a synonym for Truth. – Cease trying!
  You will not read the riddle, though you do the best you
    *can* do.

# To M. L. S —

Of all who hail thy presence as the morning –
Of all to whom thine absence is the night –
The blotting utterly from out high heaven
The sacred sun – of all who, weeping, bless thee
Hourly for hope – for life – ah, above all,
For the resurrection of deep-buried faith
In truth, in virtue, in humanity –
Of all who, on despair's unhallowed bed
Lying down to die, have suddenly arisen
At thy soft-murmured words, 'Let there be light!'
At the soft-murmured words that were fulfilled
In the seraphic glancing of thine eyes –
Of all who owe thee most, whose gratitude
Nearest resembles worship – oh, remember
The truest, the most fervently devoted,
And think that these weak lines are written by him –
By him, who, as he pens them, thrills to think
His spirit is communing with an angel's.

# Ulalume

The skies they were ashen and sober;
    The leaves they were crispéd and sere –
    The leaves they were withering and sere;
It was night in the lonesome October
    Of my most immemorial year;
It was hard by the dim lake of Auber,
    In the misty mid region of Weir –
It was down by the dank tarn of Auber,
    In the ghoul-haunted woodland of Weir.

Here once, through an alley Titanic,
    Of cypress, I roamed with my Soul –
    Of cypress, with Psyche, my Soul.
These were days when my heart was volcanic
    As the scoriac rivers that roll –
    As the lavas that restlessly roll
Their sulphurous currents down Yaanek
    In the ultimate climes of the pole –
That groan as they roll down Mount Yaanek
    In the realms of the Boreal Pole.

Our talk had been serious and sober,
    But our thoughts they were palsied and sere –
    Our memories were treacherous and sere –
For we knew not the month was October,
    And we marked not the night of the year –
    (Ah, night of all nights in the year!)
We noted not the dim lake of Auber –
    (Though once we had journeyed down here) –
Remembered not the dank tarn of Auber,
    Nor the ghoul-haunted woodland of Weir.

And now, as the night was senescent
    And star-dials pointed to morn –
    As the star-dials hinted of morn –
At the end of our path a liquescent
    And nebulous lustre was born,
Out of which a miraculous crescent
    Arose with a duplicate horn –
Astarté's bediamonded crescent
    Distinct with its duplicate horn.

And I said – 'She is warmer than Dian:
    She rolls through an ether of sighs –
    She revels in a region of sighs:
She has seen that the tears are not dry on
    These cheeks, where the worm never dies
And has come past the stars of the Lion
    To point us the path to the skies –

To the Lethean peace of the skies –
Come up, in despite of the Lion,
To shine on us with her bright eyes –
Come up through the lair of the Lion,
With love in her luminous eyes.'

But Psyche, uplifting her finger,
Said – 'Sadly this star I mistrust –
Her pallor I strangely mistrust: –
Oh, hasten! – oh, let us not linger!
Oh, fly! – let us fly! – for we must.'
In terror she spoke, letting sink her
Wings until they trailed in the dust –
In agony sobbed, letting sink her
Plumes till they trailed in the dust –
Till they sorrowfully trailed in the dust.

I replied – 'This is nothing but dreaming:
Let us on by this tremulous light!
Let us bathe in this crystalline light!
Its Sibyllic splendour is beaming
With Hope and in Beauty to-night: –
See! – it flickers up the sky through the night!
Ah, we safely may trust to its gleaming,
And be sure it will lead us aright –
We safely may trust to a gleaming
That cannot but guide us aright,
Since it flickers up to Heaven through the night.'

Thus I pacified Psyche and kissed her,
And tempted her out of her gloom –
And conquered her scruples and gloom;
And we passed to the end of the vista,
But were stopped by the door of a tomb –
By the door of a legended tomb;
And I said – 'What is written, sweet sister,
On the door of this legended tomb?'
She replied – 'Ulalume – Ulalume –
'Tis the vault of thy lost Ulalume!'

Then my heart it grew ashen and sober
    As the leaves that were crispéd and sere –
    As the leaves that were withering and sere,
And I cried – 'It was surely October
    On *this* very night of last year
    That I journeyed – I journeyed down here –
    That I brought a dread burden down here –
    On this night of all nights in the year,
    Ah, what demon has tempted me here?
Well I know, now, this dim lake of Auber –
    This misty mid region of Weir –
Well I know, now, this dank tarn of Auber,
    This ghoul-haunted woodland of Weir.'

# An Enigma

'Seldom we find,' says Solomon Don Dunce,
    'Half an idea in the profoundest sonnet.
Through all the flimsy things we see at once
    As easily as through a Naples bonnet –
    Trash of all trash! – how *can* a lady don it?
Yet heavier far than your Petrarchan stuff –
Owl-downy nonsense that the faintest puff
    Twirls into trunk-paper the while you con it.'
And, veritably, Sol is right enough.
The general tuckermanities are arrant
Bubbles – ephemeral and *so* transparent –
    But *this* is, now, – you may depend upon it –
Stable, opaque, immortal – all by dint
Of the dear names that lie concealed within 't.

# To — —

Not long ago, the writer of these lines,
In the mad pride of intellectuality,
Maintained 'the power of words' – denied that ever
A thought arose within the human brain
Beyond the utterance of the human tongue:
And now, as if in mockery of that boast,
Two words – two foreign soft dissyllables –
Italian tones, made only to be murmured
By angels dreaming in the moonlit 'dew
That hangs like chains of pearl on Hermon hill,' –
Have stirred from out the abysses of his heart,
Unthought-like thoughts that are the souls of thought,
Richer, far wilder, far diviner visions
Than even the seraph harper, Israfel,
(Who has 'the sweetest voice of all God's creatures,')
Could hope to utter. And I! my spells are broken.
The pen falls powerless from my shivering hand.
With thy dear name as text, though bidden by thee,
I cannot write – I cannot speak or think –
Alas, I cannot feel; for 'tis not feeling,
This standing motionless upon the golden
Threshold of the wide-open gate of dreams,
Gazing, entranced, adown the gorgeous vista,
And thrilling as I see, upon the right,
Upon the left, and all the way along,
Amid empurpled vapours, far away
To where the prospect terminates – *thee only*.

# The Bells

### 1
Hear the sledges with the bells –
Silver bells!
What a world of merriment their melody foretells!

How they tinkle, tinkle, tinkle,
 In the icy air of night!
While the stars that oversprinkle
All the heavens, seem to twinkle
 With a crystalline delight;
Keeping time, time, time,
In a sort of Runic rhyme,
To the tintinnabulation that so musically wells
 From the bells, bells, bells, bells,
  Bells, bells, bells –
From the jingling and the tinkling of the bells.


2

Hear the mellow wedding bells –
 Golden bells!
What a world of happiness their harmony foretells!
 Through the balmy air of night
 How they ring out their delight! –
  From the molten-golden notes,
  And all in tune,
 What a liquid ditty floats
To the turtle-dove that listens, while she gloats
 On the moon!
 Oh, from out the sounding cells,
What a gush of euphony voluminously wells!
  How it swells!
  How it dwells
 On the Future! – how it tells
 Of the rapture that impels
 To the swinging and the ringing
 Of the bells, bells, bells –
 Of the bells, bells, bells, bells,
  Bells, bells, bells –
To the rhyming and the chiming of the bells!


3

Hear the loud alarum bells –
 Brazen bells!

What a tale of terror, now, their turbulency tells!
　　In the startled ear of night
　　How they scream out their affright!
　　　Too much horrified to speak,
　　　They can only shriek, shriek,
　　　　Out of tune,
In a clamorous appealing to the mercy of the fire,
In a mad expostulation with the deaf and frantic fire,
　　　Leaping higher, higher, higher,
　　　With a desperate desire,
　　And a resolute endeavour
　　Now – now to sit, or never,
　By the side of the pale-faced moon.
　　　Oh, the bells, bells, bells!
　　　What a tale their terror tells
　　　　Of Despair!
　　How they clang, and clash, and roar!
　　What a horror they outpour
On the bosom of the palpitating air!
　　Yet the ear, it fully knows,
　　　　By the twanging,
　　　　And the clanging,
　　How the danger ebbs and flows;
　　Yet the ear distinctly tells,
　　　　In the jangling,
　　　　And the wrangling,
　　How the danger sinks and swells,
By the sinking or the swelling in the anger of the bells –
　　　　Of the bells –
　　　Of the bells, bells, bells,
　　　　Bells, bells, bells –
　In the clamour and the clangor of the bells!


4
　　Hear the tolling of the bells –
　　　Iron bells!
What a world of solemn thought their monody compels!
　　In the silence of the night,

How we shiver with affright
At the melancholy menace of their tone!
For every sound that floats
From the rust within their throats
Is a groan.
And the people – ah, the people –
They that dwell up in the steeple,
All alone,
And who, tolling, tolling, tolling,
In that muffled monotone,
Feel a glory in so rolling
On the human heart a stone –
They are neither man nor woman –
They are neither brute nor human –
They are Ghouls: –
And their king it is who tolls: –
And he rolls, rolls, rolls, rolls
A pæan from the bells!
And his merry bosom swells
With the pæan of the bells!
And he dances, and he yells;
Keeping time, time, time,
In a sort of Runic rhyme,
To the pæan of the bells: –
Of the bells:
Keeping time, time, time,
In a sort of Runic rhyme,
To the throbbing of the bells –
Of the bells, bells, bells –
To the sobbing of the bells: –
Keeping time, time, time
As he knells, knells, knells,
In a happy Runic rhyme,
To the rolling of the bells –
Of the bells, bells, bells: –
To the tolling of the bells –
Of the bells, bells, bells, bells,
Bells, bells, bells –
To the moaning and the groaning of the bells.

# To Helen

I saw thee once – once only – years ago:
I must not say *how* many – but *not* many.
It was a July midnight; and from out
A full-orbed moon, that, like thine own soul, soaring,
Sought a precipitate pathway up through heaven,
There fell a silvery-silken veil of light,
With quietude and sultriness and slumber,
Upon the upturn'd faces of a thousand
Roses that grew in an enchanted garden,
Where no wind dared to stir, unless on tiptoe –
Fell on the upturn'd faces of these roses
That gave out, in return for the love-light,
Their odorous souls in an ecstatic death –
Fell on the upturn'd faces of these roses
That smiled and died in this parterre, enchanted
By thee, and by the poetry of thy presence.

Clad all in white, upon a violet bank
I saw thee half reclining; while the moon
Fell on the upturn'd faces of the roses,
And on thine own, upturn'd – alas, in sorrow!

Was it not Fate, that, on this July midnight –
Was it not Fate, (whose name is also Sorrow,)
That bade me pause before that garden-gate,
To breathe the incense of those slumbering roses:
No footstep stirred: the hated world all slept,
Save only thee and me. (Oh, heaven! – oh, God!
How my heart beats in coupling those two words!)
Save only thee and me. I paused – I looked –
And in an instant all things disappeared.
(Ah, bear in mind this garden was enchanted!)
The pearly lustre of the moon went out:
The mossy banks and the meandering paths,
The happy flowers and the repining trees,
Were seen no more: the very roses' odours
Died in the arms of the adoring airs.

All – all expired save thee – save less than thou:
Save only the divine light in thine eyes –
Save but the soul in thine uplifted eyes.
I saw but them – they were the world to me.
I saw but them – saw only them for hours –
Saw only them until the moon went down.
What wild heart-histories seemed to lie enwritten
Upon those crystalline, celestial spheres!
How dark a wo! yet how sublime a hope!
How silently serene a sea of pride!
How daring an ambition! yet how deep –
How fathomless a capacity for love!

But now, at length, dear Dian sank from sight,
Into a western couch of thunder-cloud;
And thou, a ghost, amid the entombing trees
Didst glide away. *Only thine eyes remained*.
They *would not* go – they never yet have gone.
Lighting my lonely pathway home that night,
*They* have not left me (as my hopes have) since.
They follow me – they lead me through the years
They are my ministers – yet I their slave.
Their office is to illumine and enkindle –
My duty, *to be saved* by their bright light,
And purified in their electric fire,
And sanctified in their elysian fire.
They fill my soul with Beauty (which is Hope,)
And are far up in Heaven – the stars I kneel to
In the sad, silent watches of my night;
While even in the meridian glare of day
I see them still – two sweetly scintillant
Venuses, unextinguished by the sun!

# Eldorado

Gaily bedight,
A gallant knight,
In sunshine and in shadow,
Had journeyed long,
Singing a song,
In search of Eldorado.

But he grew old –
This knight so bold –
And o'er his heart a shadow
Fell as he found
No spot of ground
That looked like Eldorado.

And, as his strength
Failed him at length,
He met a pilgrim shadow –
'Shadow,' said he,
'Where can it be –
This land of Eldorado?'

'Over the Mountains
Of the Moon,
Down the Valley of the Shadow,
Ride, boldly ride,'
The shade replied, –
'If you seek for Eldorado.'

## For Annie

Thank Heaven! the crisis –
　　The danger is past,
And the lingering illness
　　Is over at last –
And the fever called 'Living'
　　Is conquered at last.

Sadly, I know
　　I am shorn of my strength,
And no muscle I move
　　As I lie at full length –
But no matter! – I feel
　　I am better at length.

And I rest so composedly
　　Now, in my bed,
That any beholder
　　Might fancy me dead –
Might start at beholding me,
　　Thinking me dead.

The moaning and groaning,
　　The sighing and sobbing,
Are quieted now,
　　With that horrible throbbing
At heart: – ah that horrible,
　　Horrible throbbing!

The sickness – the nausea –
　　The pitiless pain –
Have ceased with the fever
　　That maddened my brain –
With the fever called 'Living'
　　That burned in my brain.

And oh! of all tortures
　　*That* torture the worst
Has abated – the terrible

Torture of thirst
For the napthaline river
    Of Passion accurst: –
I have drank of a water
    That quenches all thirst: –

Of a water that flows,
    With a lullaby sound,
From a spring but a very few
    Feet under ground –
From a cavern not very far
    Down under ground.

And ah! let it never
    Be foolishly said
That my room it is gloomy
    And narrow my bed;
For man never slept
    In a different bed –
And, to sleep, you must slumber
    In just such a bed.

My tantalized spirit
    Here blandly reposes,
Forgetting, or never
    Regretting, its roses –
Its old agitations
    Of myrtles and roses:

For now, while so quietly
    Lying, it fancies
A holier odour
    About it, of pansies –
A rosemary odour,
    Commingled with pansies –
With rue and the beautiful
    Puritan pansies

And so it lies happily,
    Bathing in many

A dream of the truth
    And the beauty of Annie –
Drowned in a bath
    Of the tresses of Annie.

She tenderly kissed me,
    She fondly caressed,
And then I fell gently
    To sleep on her breast –
Deeply to sleep
    From the heaven of her breast.

When the light was extinguished
    She covered me warm,
And she prayed to the angels
    To keep me from harm –
To the queen of the angels
    To shield me from harm.

And I lie so composedly,
    Now, in my bed,
(Knowing her love)
    That you fancy me dead –
And I rest so contentedly,
    Now, in my bed,
(With her love at my breast)
    That you fancy me dead –
That you shudder to look at me,
    Thinking me dead: –

But my heart it is brighter
    Than all of the many
Stars of the sky,
    For it sparkles with Annie –
It glows with the light
    Of the love of my Annie –
With the thought of the light
    Of the eyes of my Annie.

# To My Mother

Because I feel that, in the Heavens above,
    The angels, whispering to one another,
Can find, among their burning terms of love,
    None so devotional as that of 'Mother',
Therefore by that dear name I long have called you –
    You who are more than mother unto me,
And fill my heart of hearts, where Death installed you,
    In setting my Virginia's spirit free.
My mother – my own mother, who died early,
    Was but the mother of myself; but you
Are mother to the one I loved so dearly,
    And thus are dearer than the mother I knew
By that infinity with which my wife
    Was dearer to my soul than its soul-life.

# Annabel Lee

It was many and many a year ago,
    In a kingdom by the sea
That a maiden there lived whom you may know
    By the name of ANNABEL LEE;
And this maiden she lived with no other thought
    Than to love and be loved by me.

I was a child and *she* was a child,
    In this kingdom by the sea,
But we loved with a love that was more than love –
    I and my ANNABEL LEE –
With a love that the wingéd seraphs of heaven
    Coveted her and me.

And this was the reason that, long ago,
    In this kingdom by the sea,

A wind blew out of a cloud, chilling
    My beautiful ANNABEL LEE;
So that her highborn kinsmen came
    And bore her away from me,
To shut her up in a sepulchre
    In this kingdom by the sea.

The angels, not half so happy in heaven,
    Went envying her and me –
Yes! – that was the reason (as all men know,
    In this kingdom by the sea)
That the wind came out of the cloud by night,
    Chilling and killing my ANNABEL LEE.

But our love it was stronger by far than the love
    Of those who were older than we –
    Of many far wiser than we –
And neither the angels in heaven above,
    Nor the demons down under the sea,
Can ever dissever my soul from the soul
    Of the beautiful ANNABEL LEE:

For the moon never beams, without bringing me dreams
    Of the beautiful ANNABEL LEE;
And the stars never rise, but I feel the bright eyes
    Of the beautiful ANNABEL LEE;
And so, all the night-tide, I lie down by the side
Of my darling – my darling – my life and my bride,
    In her sepulchre there by the sea –
    In her tomb by the sounding sea.

## *from* **The Philosophy of Composition**

*

The initial consideration [in writing 'The Raven'] was that of extent. If any literary work is too long to be read at one sitting, we must be content to dispense with the immensely important effect derivable from unity of impression – for, if two sittings be required, the affairs of the world interfere, and everything like totality is at once destroyed. But since, *ceteris paribus*, no poet can afford to dispense with *anything* that may advance his design, it remains to be seen whether there is, in extent, any advantage to counterbalance the loss of unity which attends it. Here I say no, at once. What we term a long poem is, in fact, merely a succession of brief ones – that is to say, of brief poetical effects. It is needless to demonstrate that a poem is such, only inasmuch as it intensely excites, by elevating, the soul; and all intense excitements are, through a psychal necessity, brief.

*

Holding in view these considerations, as well as that degree of excitement which I deemed not above the popular, while not below the critical, taste, I reached at once what I conceived the proper length for my intended poem – a length of about one hundred lines. It is, in fact, a hundred and eight.

My next thought concerned the choice of an impression, or effect, to be conveyed; and here I may well observe that, throughout the construction, I kept steadily in view the design of rendering the work *universally* appreciable. I should be carried too far out of my immediate topic were I to demonstrate a point upon which I have repeatedly insisted, and which, with the poetical, stands not in the slightest need of demonstration – the point, I mean, that Beauty is the sole legitimate province of the poem.

*

Regarding, then, Beauty as my province, my next question referred to the *tone* of its highest manifestation – and all experience has shown that this tone is one of *sadness*. Beauty of whatever kind, in its supreme development, invariably excites the sensitive soul to tears. Melancholy is thus the most legitimate of all the poetical tones.

The length, the province, and the tone, being thus determined, I betook myself to ordinary induction, with the view of obtaining some artistic piquancy which might serve me as a key-note in the construction of the poem – some pivot upon which the whole structure might turn. In carefully thinking over all the usual artistic effects – or more properly *points*, in the theatrical sense – I did not fail to perceive immediately that no one had been so universally employed as that of the *refrain*. The universality of its employment sufficed to assure me of its intrinsic value, and spared me the necessity of submitting it to analysis. I considered it, however, with regard to its susceptibility of improvement, and soon saw it to be in a primitive condition. As commonly used, the *refrain*, or burden, not only is limited to lyric verse, but depends for its impression upon the force of monotone – both in sound and thought. The pleasure is deduced solely from the sense of identity – of repetition. I resolved to diversify, and so heighten, the effect, by adhering, in general, to the monotone of sound, while I continually varied that of thought: that is to say, I determined to produce continuously novel effects, by the *variation of the application* of the *refrain* – the *refrain* itself remaining, for the most part, unvaried.

These points being settled, I next bethought me of the *nature* of my *refrain*. Since its application was to be repeatedly varied, it was clear that the *refrain* itself must be brief, for there would have been an insurmountable difficulty in frequent variations of application in any sentence of length. In proportion of the brevity of the sentence, would, of course, be the facility of the *variation*. This led me at once to a single word as the best *refrain*.

The question now arose as to the *character* of the word. Having made up my mind to a *refrain*, the division of the poem into stanzas was, of course, a corollary: the *refrain* forming the close to each stanza. That such a close, to have force, must be sonorous and susceptible of protracted emphasis, admitted no doubt: and these considerations inevitably led me to the long *o* as the most sonorous vowel, in connection with *r* as the most producible consonant.

The sound of the *refrain* being thus determined, it became necessary to select a word embodying this sound, and at the same time in the fullest possible keeping with that melancholy which I had predetermined as the tone of the poem. In such a search it would have been absolutely impossible to overlook the word 'Nevermore'. In fact, it was the very first which presented itself.

*

I had now gone so far as the conception of a Raven – the bird of ill omen – monotonously repeating the one word, 'Nevermore', at the conclusion of each stanza, in a poem of melancholy tone, and in length about one hundred lines. Now, never losing sight of the object *supremeness*, or perfection, at all points, I asked myself – 'Of all melancholy topics, what, according to the *universal* understanding of mankind, is the *most* melancholy?' Death – was the obvious reply. 'And when,' I said, 'is this most melancholy of topics most poetical?' From what I have already explained at some length, the answer, here also, is obvious – 'When it most closely allies itself to *Beauty*: the death, then, of a beautiful woman is, unquestionably, the most poetical topic in the world – and equally is it beyond doubt that the lips best suited for such topic are those of a bereaved lover.'

I had now to combine the two ideas, of a lover lamenting his deceased mistress and a Raven continuously repeating the word 'Nevermore'. – I had to combine these, bearing in mind my design of varying at every turn, the *application* of the word repeated; but the only intelligible mode of such combination is that of imagining the Raven employing the word in answer to the queries of the lover. And here it was that I saw at once the opportunity afforded for the effect on which I had been depending – that is to say, the effect of the *variation of application*. I saw that I could make the first query propounded by the lover – the first query to which the Raven should reply 'Nevermore' – that I could make this first query a commonplace one – the second less so – the third still less, and so on – until at length the lover, startled from his original *nonchalance* by the melancholy character of the word itself – by its frequent repetition – and by a consideration of the ominous reputation of the fowl that uttered it – is at length excited to superstition, and wildly propounds queries of a far different character – queries whose solution he has passionately at heart – propounds them half in superstition and half in that species of despair which delights in self-torture – propounds them not altogether because he believes in the prophetic or demoniac character of the bird (which, reason assures him, is merely repeating a lesson learned by rote) but because he experiences a frenzied pleasure in so modelling his questions as to receive from the *expected* 'Nevermore' the most delicious because the most intolerable of sorrow. Perceiving the opportunity thus afforded me – or, more strictly, thus forced upon me in the progress of the construction – I first established in mind the climax, or concluding query – that query to which 'Nevermore' should be in the last place an answer – that query in reply to which this word 'Nevermore' should involve the utmost conceivable amount of sorrow and despair.

Here then the poem may be said to have its beginning – at the end, where all works of art should begin – for it was here, at this point of my preconsiderations, that I first put pen to paper, in the composition of the stanza:

> 'Prophet,' said I, 'thing of evil! prophet still if bird or devil!
> By that heaven that bends above us – by that God we both adore,
> Tell this soul with sorrow laden, if within the distant Aidenn,
> I shall clasp a sainted maiden whom the angels name Lenore –
> Clasp a rare and radiant maiden whom the angels name Lenore.'
>               Quoth the raven 'Nevermore.'

I composed this stanza, at this point, first that, by establishing the climax, I might the better vary and graduate, as regards seriousness and importance, the preceding queries of the lover – and, secondly, that I might definitely settle the rhythm, the metre, and the length and general arrangement of the stanza – as well as graduate the stanzas which were to precede, so that none of them might surpass this in rhythmical effect. Had I been able, in the subsequent composition, to construct more vigorous stanzas, I should, without scruple, have purposely enfeebled them, so as not to interfere with the climacteric effect.

*

## *from* **The Poetic Principle**

*

I need scarcely observe that a poem deserves its title only inasmuch as it excites, by elevating the soul. The value of the poem is in the ratio of this elevating excitement. But all excitements are, through a psychal necessity, transient. That degree of excitement which would entitle a poem to be so called at all, cannot be sustained throughout a composition of any great length. After the lapse of half an hour, at the very utmost, it flags – fails – a revulsion ensues – and then the poem is, in effect, and in fact, no longer such.

There are, no doubt, many who have found difficulty in reconciling the critical dictum that the *Paradise Lost* is to be devoutly admired throughout, with the absolute impossibility of maintaining for it, during perusal, the amount of enthusiasm which that critical dictum would demand. This great work, in fact, is to be regarded as poetical, only when, losing sight of that vital requisite in all works of Art, Unity, we view it merely as a series of minor poems. If, to preserve its Unity – its totality of effect or impression – we read it (as would be necessary) at a single sitting, the result is but a constant alternation of excitement and depression. After a passage of what we feel to be true poetry, there follows, inevitably, a passage of platitude which no critical pre-judgment can force us to admire; but if, upon completing the work, we read it again; omitting the first book – that is to say, commencing with the second – we shall be surprised at now finding that admirable which we before condemned – that damnable which we had previously so much admired. It follows from all this that the ultimate, aggregate, or absolute effect of even the best epic under the sun, is a nullity: – and this is precisely the fact.

*

On the other hand, it is clear that a poem may be improperly brief. Undue brevity degenerates into mere epigrammatism. A *very* short poem, while now and then producing a brilliant or vivid, never produces a profound or enduring effect. There must be the steady pressing down of the stamp upon the wax. De Béranger has wrought innumerable things, pungent and spirit-stirring; but, in general, they have been too imponderous to stamp themselves

deeply into the public attention; and thus, as so many feathers of
fancy, have been blown aloft only to be whistled down the wind.

*

While the epic mania – while the idea that, to merit in poetry,
prolixity is indispensable – has, for some years past, been gradually
dying out of the public mind, by mere dint of its own absurdity – we
find it succeeded by a heresy too palpably false to be long tolerated,
but one which, in the brief period it has already endured, may be
said to have accomplished more in the corruption of our Poetical
Literature than all its other enemies combined. I allude to the
heresy of *The Didactic*. It has been assumed, tacitly and avowedly,
directly and indirectly, that the ultimate object of all Poetry is
Truth. Every poem, it is said, should inculcate a moral; and by this
moral is the poetical merit of the work to be adjudged. We
Americans especially have patronized this happy idea; and we
Bostonians, very especially, have developed it in full. We have
taken it into our heads that to write a poem simply for the poem's
sake, and to acknowledge such to have been our design, would be
to confess ourselves radically wanting in the true Poetic dignity and
force: – but the simple fact is, that, would we but permit ourselves to
look into our own souls, we should immediately there discover that
under the sun there neither exists nor *can* exist any work more
thoroughly dignified – more supremely noble than this very poem –
this poem *per se* – this poem which is a poem and nothing more –
this poem written solely for the poem's sake.

With as deep a reverence for the True as ever inspired the bosom
of man, I would, nevertheless, limit, in some measure, its modes of
inculcation. I would limit to enforce them. I would not enfeeble
them by dissipation. The demands of Truth are severe. She has no
sympathy with the myrtles. All *that* which is so indispensable in
Song, is precisely all *that* with which *she* has nothing whatever to
do. It is but making her a flaunting paradox, to wreathe her in gems
and flowers. In enforcing a truth, we need severity rather than
efflorescence of language. We must be simple, precise, terse. We
must be cool, calm, unimpassioned. In a word, we must be in that
mood which, as nearly as possible, is the exact converse of the
poetical. *He* must be blind indeed who does not perceive the radical
and chasmal differences between the truthful and the poetical
modes of inculcation. He must be theory-mad beyond redemption

who, in spite of these differences, shall still persist in attempting to reconcile the obstinate oils and waters of Poetry and Truth.

Dividing the world of mind into its three most immediately obvious distinctions, we have the Pure Intellect, Taste, and the Moral Sense. I place Taste in the middle, because it is just this position which, in the mind, it occupies. It holds intimate relations with either extreme; but from the Moral Sense is separated by so faint a difference that Aristotle has not hesitated to place some of its operations among the virtues themselves. Nevertheless, we find the *offices* of the trio marked with a sufficient distinction. Just as the Intellect concerns itself with Truth, so Taste informs us of the Beautiful while the Moral Sense is regardful of Duty. Of this latter, while Conscience teaches the obligation, and Reason the expediency, Taste contents herself with displaying the charms: – waging war upon Vice solely on the ground of her deformity – her disproportion – her animosity to the fitting, to the appropriate, to the harmonious – in a word, to Beauty.

An immortal instinct, deep within the spirit of man, is thus, plainly, a sense of the Beautiful. This it is which administers to his delight in the manifold forms, and sounds, and odours, and sentiments amid which he exists. And just as the lily is repeated in the lake, or the eyes of Amaryllis in the mirror, so is the mere oral or written repetition of these forms, and sounds, and colours, and odours, and sentiments, a duplicate source of delight. But this mere repetition is not poetry. He who shall simply sing, with however glowing enthusiasm, or with however vivid a truth of description, of the sights, and sounds, and odours, and colours, and sentiments, which greet *him* in common with all mankind – he, I say, has yet failed to prove his divine title. There is still a something in the distance which he has been unable to attain. We have still a thirst unquenchable, to allay which he has not shown us the crystal springs. This thirst belongs to the immortality of Man. It is at once a consequence and an indication of his perennial existence. It is the desire of the moth for the star. It is no mere appreciation of the Beauty before us – but a wild effort to reach the Beauty above. Inspired by an ecstatic prescience of the glories beyond the grave, we struggle, by multiform combinations among the things and thoughts of Time, to attain a portion of that Loveliness whose very elements, perhaps, appertain to eternity alone. And thus when by Poetry – or when by Music, the most entrancing of the Poetic moods – we find ourselves melted into tears – we weep then – not as the Abbaté Gravina supposes – through excess of pleasure, but through a certain, petulant, impatient sorrow at our inability to grasp *now*, wholly, here on earth, at once and for ever, those divine and rapturous joys, of which *through* the poem, or *through* the music, we attain to but brief and indeterminate glimpses.

The struggle to apprehend the supernal Loveliness – this struggle, on the part of souls fittingly constituted – has given to the world all *that* which it (the world) has ever been enabled at once to understand and *to feel* as poetic.

The Poetic Sentiment, of course, may develop itself in various modes – in Painting, in Sculpture, in Architecture, in the Dance – very especially in Music – and very peculiarly, and with a wide field, in the composition of the Landscape Garden. Our present theme, however, has regard only to its manifestation in words. And here let me speak briefly on the topic of rhythm. Contenting myself with the certainty that Music, in its various modes of metre, rhythm, and rhyme, is of so vast a moment in Poetry as never to be wisely rejected – is so vitally important an adjunct, that he is simply silly who declines its assistance, I will not now pause to maintain its absolute essentiality. It is in Music, perhaps, that the soul most nearly attains the great end for which, when inspired by the Poetic Sentiment, it struggles – the creation of supernal Beauty. It *may* be, indeed, that here this sublime end is, now and then, attained *in fact*. We are often made to feel, with a shivering delight, that from an earthly harp are stricken notes which *cannot* have been unfamiliar to the angels. And thus there can be little doubt that in the union of Poetry with Music in its popular sense, we shall find the widest field for the Poetic development. The old Bards and Minnesingers had advantages which we do not possess – and Thomas Moore, singing his own songs, was, in the most legitimate manner, perfecting them as poems.

To recapitulate, then: – I would define, in brief, the Poetry of words as *The Rhythmical Creation of Beauty*. Its sole arbiter is Taste. With the Intellect or with the Conscience, it has only collateral relations. Unless incidentally, it has no concern whatever either with Duty or with Truth.

A few words, however, in explanation. *That* pleasure which is at once the most pure, the most elevating, and the most intense, is derived, I maintain, from the contemplation of the Beautiful. In the contemplation of Beauty we alone find it possible to attain that pleasurable elevation, or excitement, *of the soul*, which we recognize as the Poetic Sentiment, and which is so easily distinguished from Truth, which is the satisfaction of the Reason, or from Passion, which is the excitement of the heart. I make Beauty, therefore – using the word as inclusive of the sublime – I make Beauty the province of the poem, simply because it is an obvious rule of Art that effects should be made to spring as directly as possible from their causes: – no one as yet having been weak enough to deny that the peculiar elevation in question is at least *most readily* attainable in the poem. It by no means follows, however, that the incitements of Passion, or the precepts of Duty, or even the lessons of Truth, may not be introduced into a poem, and with advantage; for they may subserve, incidentally, in various ways, the general purposes of the work: – but the true artist will always contrive to tone them down in proper subjection to that *Beauty* which is the atmosphere and the real essence of the poem.

*

Thus, although in a very cursory and imperfect manner, I have endeavoured to convey to you my conception of the Poetic Principle. It has been my purpose to suggest that, while this Principle itself is, strictly and simply, the Human Aspiration for Supernal Beauty, the manifestation of the Principle is always found in an *elevating excitement of the Soul* – quite independent of that passion which is the intoxication of the Heart – or of that Truth which is the satisfaction of the Reason. For, in regard to Passion, alas! its tendency is to degrade, rather than to elevate the Soul. Love, on the contrary – Love – the true, the divine Eros – the Uranian, as distinguished from the Dionæan Venus – is unquestionably the purest and truest of all poetical themes. And in regard to Truth – if, to be sure, through the attainment of a truth, we are led to perceive a harmony where none was apparent before, we experience, at once, the true poetical effect – but this effect is referable to the harmony alone, and not in the least degree to the truth which merely served to render the harmony manifest.

We shall reach, however, more immediately a distinct conception of what the true Poetry is, by mere reference to a few of the simple elements which induce in the Poet himself the true poetical effect. He recognizes the ambrosia which nourishes his soul, in the bright orbs that shine in Heaven – in the volutes of the flower – in the clustering of low shrubberies – in the waving of the grain-fields – in the slanting of tall, Eastern trees – in the blue distance of mountains – in the grouping of clouds – in the twinkling of half-hidden brooks – in the gleaming of silver rivers – in the repose of sequestered lakes – in the star-mirroring depths of lonely wells. He perceives it in the songs of birds – in the harp of Æolus – in the sighing of the night-wind – in the repining voice of the forest – in the surf that complains to the shore – in the fresh breath of the woods – in the scent of the violet – in the voluptuous perfume of the hyacinth – in the suggestive odour that comes to him, at eventide, from far-distant, undiscovered islands, over dim oceans, illimitable and unexplored. He owns it in all noble thoughts – in all unworldly motives – in all holy impulses – in all chivalrous, generous, and self-sacrificing deeds. He feels it in the beauty of woman – in the grace of her step – in the lustre of her eye – in the melody of her voice – in her soft laughter – in her sigh – in the harmony of the rustling of her robes. He deeply feels it in her winning endearments – in her burning enthusiasms – in her gentle charities – in her meek and devotional endurances – but above all – ah, far above all – he kneels to it – he worships it in the faith, in the purity, in the strength, in the altogether divine majesty – of her *love*.

*

# Notes

## Poems

***Tamerlane:*** Poe took little from the historical sources concerning Tamerlane (1336–1405). His poem is more of a lyric allegory, based on his love for Sarah Elmira Royster. Engaged to her, Poe left for the University of Virginia. Although he wrote home to her, her father intercepted the letters; and Poe returned to Richmond to find her engaged to someone else and therefore 'dead' to him.

***To —— :*** This evidently refers to the marriage of Sarah Elmira Royster to someone else.

***Dreams:*** This early poem reveals Poe's poetic debt to Byron.

***Spirits of the Dead:*** An earlier version of this poem was entitled 'Visit of the Dead'. This is an early example of one of Poe's favourite subjects, the 'imaginative landscape'.

***Evening Star:*** This poem anticipates 'Ulalume'.

***A Dream Within a Dream:*** This was originally entitled 'Imitation', possibly in acknowledgement of its indebtedness to Byron.

***Stanzas:*** This relatively difficult poem describes how in youth the poet communed with nature but did not understand its 'power'. He questions if this is madness but believes it is visionary. Finding deep meaning in commonplace things, he declares that beauty, anticipating heaven, draws him away from a fall threatened by pride. The epigraph is from Byron's *The Island*, II. xvi. 13–16.

***A Dream:*** This poem probably alludes to the poet's loss of Mrs Stanard ('Helen') and Sarah Elmira Royster.

***'The Happiest Day, the Happiest Hour':*** Also indebted to Byron (as are so many of Poe's verses), this poem may refer to the 'happiest day' when, privately at least, Poe became engaged to Sarah Elmira Royster.

*The Lake: To —* : This is based on a visit Poe made at sunset to the Lake of the Dismal Swamp in Virginia.

*Sonnet – To Science:* This sonnet, in which Poe declares his aim of disregarding scientific fact when imaginative fantasy seems more compelling, was first used as an introduction to *Al Aaraaf, Tamerlane, and Minor Poems* (1829) and then served as a motto to the prose fantasy, *The Island of Fay.*

*Al Aaraaf:* In the Koran, Al Aaraaf is the name Mohammedans give to the middle kingdom between heaven and hell (cf. limbo). Its inhabitants were tantalized by being offered glimpses of paradise. The main theme of the poem concerning the nature and divinity of beauty is supplemented by a subsidiary theme highlighting the power of knowledge to spoil human appreciation of that beauty.

*Romance:* A declaration of the poet's dedication to romance in the voice of nature (a voice speaking to him through a parakeet), this poem was originally titled 'Preface'.

*To —* : This poem may be seen as an early version of 'A Dream Within a Dream'. It is not certain who the subject of the poem is, although Poe's cousin, Elizabeth Herring, has been suggested.

*To the River —* : There is a concealed joke here, in that the poem alludes to Byron's 'Stanza to the Po', with 'Po' (a river in Italy) being a play on the author's name.

*To —* : Originally entitled 'To M—' (in a different version), the subject of this poem is unknown.

*Fairy-Land:* Another example of Poe's interest in imaginative landscapes, this poem mixes fantasy with touches of arch humour.

*To Helen:* Poe took twelve years to perfect this poem, often regarded as the finest of his lyrics. In a letter written in 1848, he confessed that it was inspired by 'the first purely ideal love of my soul': Mrs Jane Stith Stanard whom he had known during his youth in Richmond. Poe uses this personal memory as the basis for celebrating beauty and the spiritual love that leads us to that beauty, guiding us out of the mundane and commonplace and into 'the regions which/Are Holy Land!'

**Israfel:** This poem is inspired by a passage from the Koran: 'And the angel Israfel, whose heart-strings are a lute, and who has the sweetest voice of all God's creatures'.

**The City in the Sea:** One of the most famous of Poe's poems, this is discussed in the introduction. An earlier version was entitled 'The Doomed City'.

**The Sleeper:** The original version of this poem was entitled 'Irene'. It illustrates Poe's interest in the death of beautiful women, which in *The Philosophy of Composition* he termed 'the most poetical topic in the world'.

**Lenore:** The very earliest version of this was entitled *Pæan*.

**The Valley of Unrest:** Entitled in its original version 'The Valley of Nis', this poem is another example of the subject he made his own, the imaginative landscape. 'Distant subjects,' Poe wrote in his notes for a projected book on American writers, 'are in fact the most desirable . . . The true poet is less affected by the absolute contemplation than the imagination of a great landscape.'

**The Coliseum:** For Poe, in this poem, the Colosseum in Rome is both a memorial to the sources of our civilization and an inspiration for the present and future.

**To One in Paradise:** In his tale *The Visionary*, subsequently entitled 'The Assignation', Poe presents this poem as the composition of the protagonist whose beloved is married to an older nobleman.

**Hymn:** Addressed to the Virgin Mary, this is Poe's most overtly religious poem.

**To F——:** This is one of three poems to Mrs Frances Sargent Osgood, the other two being To F — s S. O—d and *A Valentine*. Mrs Osgood was one of the women with whom Poe had a close relationship in the later part of his life.

***To F — s S. O — d:*** An earlier version of this poem was entitled 'Lines Written in an Album'.

***Scenes from* Politian:** The plot of *Politian* is drawn from a sensational series of events occurring in Kentucky in 1825 and 1826. Jeroboam O. Beauchamp murdered the man who betrayed Beauchamp's wife, a Colonel Solomon P. Sharp. Beauchamp was tried and convicted; Beauchamp's wife committed suicide; and Beauchamp then attempted to commit suicide on the day scheduled for his execution. The names of Poe's dramatis personæ are drawn from Italian history: characteristically, he distanced what became known as 'the Kentucky tragedy' by situating it in a different time and place.

***Bridal Ballad:*** This poem may refer to the marriage of Sarah Elmira Royster to someone else, and to her distress at learning that Poe had not, as she had believed, been disloyal while away from her.

***Sonnet to Zante:*** Zante is a modern form of Zacynthus, an island whose name has associations with the hyacinth, 'fairest of all flowers'. The occasion of this poem may have been a meeting between Poe and his new wife Virginia, with an old sweetheart of Poe's, Elmira Shelton, now married to another.

***The Haunted Palace:*** This poem is clearly an allegory, describing a person with golden hair, bright eyes, fine teeth and lips, full of intelligent and poetic utterances, who is seized by madness; his eyes consequently become bloodshot, his whole physical being deteriorates, and only insane laughter issues from his lips. In *The Fall of the House of Usher*, the poem is attributed to Roderick Usher who is, by this means, alluding to his own strange decline.

***Sonnet – Silence:*** A poem that explores the silences of nature in its apparently virgin state, this also contrasts death of the body, which is inevitable, with death of the soul, which is not.

***The Conqueror Worm:*** In its second version, this poem was included in the tale *Ligeia*. One commentator has suggested that its five stanzas represent or correspond to the five acts of a tragedy.

***Dream-Land:*** As a variation on the theme of the imaginative landscape, this is close to some earlier poems, like 'Spirits of the Dead', 'Valley of Unrest', and 'Fairy-Land'. In its constant use of a refrain, however, it is close to some later poems, such as 'Eulalie – A Song', 'The Raven', and 'Ulalume'.

**The Raven:** Poe regarded this poem as his masterpiece and discussed it at length in 'The Philosophy of Composition'. For further details see both that essay and the introduction.

**Eulalie – A Song:** It is not known if there was any specific woman to whom this poem was addressed. It may have been written for Virginia Poe; the name was probably chosen for its musicality.

**A Valentine:** The name of the person to whom this poem is addressed is concealed in the lines. By combining the first letter of the first line with the second letter of the second line, and so on, the reader will come up with the name, Frances Sargent Osgood.

**To M. L. S — :** This is a tribute to Mrs Marie Louise Shaw, who nursed Poe and his wife Virginia when they were ill.

**Ulalume:** This poem, probably written only a few weeks before Poe's death, belongs to a genre of dialogues between body and soul that were popular during the Middle Ages. It describes how, in October of a year when recollection is difficult, in the imaginary world of music and painting the protagonist and his soul walk through a mysterious landscape. It is Hallowe'en, when the dead have power, and as dawn draws near they see the planet of love in the sky: that planet is seen as warmer than the moon and as having escaped from the turmoil of lust. The soul does not trust Venus but is soothed by reasoning until they stop at a tomb, which is that of the protagonist's lost love. A question is posed as to whether the ghouls, friendly to living people, have summoned up a phantom of hope to rescue the walkers from memory of a terrible loss.

The title of the poem may be taken from the Latin verb *ululare* (to wail); and the details of the journey may recall walks taken by Poe to visit the grave of his wife Virginia.

**An Enigma:** The name of Sarah Anna Lewis, a close friend of Poe's, can be constructed by combining the first letter of the first line with the second letter of the second line, and so on.

***To* ——:** The subject of this poem is Marie Louise Shaw (see 'To M. L. S—') whose forenames are 'two foreign soft dissyllables.'

***The Bells:*** This poem has often been praised for its use of onomatopœia, repetition, assonance, and alliteration and, in general, for its attempt to turn language into music.

***To Helen:*** This poem describes Poe's romantic love affair with Sarah Helen Whitman. Poe claimed that he first saw Sarah Whitman in 1845. Later, he proposed marriage to her; and she agreed, it seems, on the understanding that he would abstain from alcohol. The banns were read: but, on the day before the wedding, Sarah Whitman heard that Poe had not kept his pledge and broke off the engagement.

***Eldorado:*** Sometimes described as Poe's last poem, this takes the legendary realm of Eldorado, a land of gold that is sought but never found, and links it with the occasion of the 1849 Gold Rush to California. Characteristically, Poe attempts to transform a historical moment into a spiritual legend.

***For Annie:*** This is addressed to a close and long-time friend of Poe's, Mrs Annie Richmond, from whom, Poe claimed, he had extracted the promise that she would come to him on his 'bed of death'.

***To My Mother:*** This poem is, in fact, addressed to Poe's mother-in-law, Mrs Maria Clemm.

***Annabel Lee:*** Although there have been several different claims as to the subject of this poem, it is commonly accepted that it refers to Virginia, Poe's wife.

## Essays

***The Philosophy of Composition:*** For a discussion of this essay, see the introduction. The title could be paraphrased as 'The Theory of Writing'.

***The Poetic Principle:*** Probably the most intensive and sustained discussion of the poetic art that Poe ever wrote, this essay is discussed in the introduction.